to me

c

BM

ID0467235

12 . 15

Voyages of the Damn Foole

Voyages of the

Damn Foole

tom mcgrath

International Marine
Camden, Maine

International Marine/
Ragged Mountain Press

A Division of The McGraw-Hill Companies

10 9 8 7 6 5 4 3 2 1

Library of Congress Cataloging-in-Publication Data
McGrath, Tom, 1931–
      Voyages of the Damn Foole / Tom McGrath.
        p.   cm.
      ISBN 0-07-045089-7 (acid-free paper)
      I. Title.
    PS3563.C3666V69   1997
    813'.54—DC21

Questions regarding the content of this book should be addressed to:
International Marine
P.O. Box 220
Camden, ME 04843

Questions regarding the ordering of this book should be addressed to:
McGraw-Hill, Inc.
Customer Service Department
P.O. Box 547
Blacklick, OH 43004
Retail customers: 1-800-262-4729
Bookstores: 1-800-233-4726

Voyages of the Damn Foole was typeset in 10 pt Weiss

Printed by R. R. Donnelley and Sons, Crawfordsville, IN
Design and Production by Dan Kirchoff
Edited by Jonathan Eaton, Kathryn Mallien

Contents

Flight of the Damn Foole

INSURED?

"By the way," I asked my wife, "am I insured?"

"No," was her acerbic reply, "we couldn't afford the payments."

"Then if I disappear on this trip don't bother looking for me. You can't afford to do anything with the remains," I said.

"What happens to us if you don't come back?" she asked. "I mean, who'll pay the bills?"

"Why worry? They're not being paid now."

The Dog staggered around the house, falling down occasionally. He was finished. His pills weren't working anymore. I had to take him to the vet to be put away. In the office of the vet I agonized through the paperwork for his euthanasia while he nuzzled up against my leg, making me wish I could have taken his place.

DOG

I paid the bill and went to a camping store to buy things for a two-week cruise. I soon realized that I couldn't afford anything there with the money I had left. From there I went to a food discount store and bought beans, juice, oatmeal, crackers,

peanuts, granola, etc. Out in the parking lot a little old lady backed her little old vintage car into my little old vintage car. I wired her bumper up with a coathanger. We smiled at each other and happily drove off to avoid the insurance claims.

STORE

AFTER THE ACCIDENT I'm telling you all this unrelated stuff to show you all the unrelated problems you'll encounter while "Fitting Out." During the winter I tried to think of something intelligent to paint on the hull. I tried hard but my intelligence failed me. So I opened a can of paint and dipped into it and let the brush do whatever it wanted to do. Later, people got mad when they tried to describe it. They would start off, "It looks like . . ." and then couldn't finish.

Then I laid the old stained sails on the grass and threw green tie-dye on them, let them set a while, then hung them

1

GREEN SAILS

up to dry. The neighbors asked, "Why did you do that?"

"How the hell do I know?" I had to answer.

I threw everything into trashbags and drove to the Dory Club in my 1962 Dodge that was long overdue for euthanasia. Five wharf rats were waiting for me, standing on the dock like barnacles on a rock. Word had gotten around that I was going to sail my Townie to Nova Scotia. I avoided them. I didn't want to be subjected to their amiable jokes. I didn't feel very amiable after what I did to the Dog.

BARNACLES

I pulled someone's pram from the rack and loaded it. The wharf rats watched and offered no help. Not that I expected, or wanted, any. "Fitting Out" is a very personal thing and a special state of mind goes along with the doing of it. I made three trips and found that each time I left on a

3 TRIPS

trip I brought less and less, but less always manages to fill up the boat. I was more concerned with what I wanted to leave ashore. Bills, a broken-down car, a broken-down house, a job, my memory, my

LESS

obnoxious self, a dead dog that I liked to walk with through the woods even if he didn't like the trees. I wanted to leave my growing revulsion for people, which was beginning to scare me. Yes, I was in flight. To lose myself on the sea.

"How long are we going for?" the boat asked.

"Two weeks," I answered as I bailed. I have to get a bigger bailing bucket each year to stay afloat.

FLIGHT

BAILING BUCKETS

The boat rolled rhythmically on the swells that broke on the nearby beach. It felt good to be sitting in the boat. It was mid-season, and we were the only Townie in the water. During the winter the fleet had been over-administrated with too many plans and too many rules. That delicate enthusiasm was gone. The fleet was in decline.

ONLY TOWNIE

STARTING OUT

When I raised the sails I discovered that I had put the luff on the boom and the foot on the mast. The boat chuckled, "That'll give those wharf rats something to talk about." I would have liked to straighten out the spreaders. They were cockeyed, but I didn't dare go into the dock.

"Fix 'em later," I told myself. "Straighten this messy boat out, too."

A gentle easterly wind brought a little rain as we tacked out of the harbor. The H.M.S. *Bounty* was just leaving Boston Harbor under full sail. I felt that I was dropped back in time to 1789. "I should sail after it and climb aboard."

H.M.S. BOUNTY

"No," the boat said, "you'd be a mutineer."

We turned away on a reach with a beam sea rolling us. At Swampscott I could hear the band playing, reminding me that it was the Fourth of July. The marchers paraded about, overjoyed that they had slaughtered the enemy by the thousands in a recent conflict. Better them than us, was the sentiment. I stood up and began ranting.

(The boat suggests that the reader skip the following paragraphs because they may contain objectionable material!)

"You politicians can cheat, lie, scheme, cajole, plead, weep and generally bullshit your way into getting elected. But you can't function at all when it comes time for avoiding a war. You can only threaten, bully, demand, spy, and kill. You want us to be patriotic, yet you've robbed our banks, ruined our economy, chased our industry away, encouraged imports, left us unemployed and overtaxed, cut education and health care, done nothing for the environment, threw the insane and homeless into the streets, ignored the elderly, crime, AIDS, pollution, and cancer. Then you gave yourselves a raise.

"Yet every politician boasts he has the solution to one of these problems. Surprisingly, the problem is never solved. It gets him elected the next time. Try to unseat one of these politicians and he'll laugh at you, because he knows elections are a joke and that your vote has as much value as a lottery ticket. Politicians don't represent us, they represent themselves. Periodically they explain what they want us to do. And what they wanted us to do this past winter was to start killing others—after we taught our kids that killing is wrong and that to be a good member of society we should avoid conflict and try to be polite and kind to one another. Now the politicians want to train our kids to kill. To run in a murderous pack. They tell them it's heroic and that if they kill enough they'll get medals and be able to march in the parade on the Fourth of July. If our pet dogs were taken to be trained like this we would be more outraged.

CELEBRATE THE KILLING ——

"If we can't see that all wars are blundered into by these political disfunctionaries and that all the misery and slaughter is useless, then our society is a total failure. We've found endless reasons to kill. We're supposed to try like hell not to, even when we're threatened. Religions were based on pacifism; 'Thou shalt not kill' is the rule we ignore. Maybe all our churches should be padlocked to stop this beastliness. Otherwise we'll wave the flags and shout patriotic inanities while marching off for another grand bloodletting. Perhaps for no reason at all, just for the hell of it."

"Are you through?" the boat asked.

"Yes," I replied proudly.

"Good. Now sit down and shut up. I couldn't stand much more of that!"

Off Marblehead we sailed through the Halifax Race fleet.

Preparing to start, they looked like baby carriages and bath-

BABY CARRIAGES AND BATHTUBS

tubs improved by space technology to make them super-raceable. Large cruising boats motored by us like pelagic condos.

We sailed close to the mysterious platform off Gloucester Harbor. Omnivorous Gloucester, sending boats out night and day to ravage the oceans. Independent of nature, they are more like trucks picking up and

MYSTERY

LOST AT SEA

delivering fish seven days a week. They're the ones who should be in church. "Give nature a little respite!"

"You're a fine one to talk of church," the boat said.

"For others. As for me, I'd rather be lost at sea than found in church."

We rounded Cape Ann on the run. Halibut Point and Folly Cove. Through the hole-in-the-wall into Lanesville. I dropped the anchor from the stern and rowed to the breakwater to tie the bowline. (This sounds neat,

HOLE IN THE WALL

but it never works right for me. I usually keep changing it and then leave it whichever way it is when I get disgusted.) I laid out the sleeping bag, set up the sail tent, and cooked some beans. Looking forward to a nice breakfast in the morning at the diner ashore, I slept, complaining through my dreams.

Next morning I stowed everything away, got the boat ready for sailing, and walked ashore to the diner. The board of health

had closed it down. Back aboard, I made oatmeal. It went down like cement and stayed in my stomach the whole day. With food I have to admit

OATMEAL to being slightly peculiar. I don't like eating. I like only the smell of food. As far as I am

concerned, food should be cooked, smelled, and then thrown away. Avoiding the elaborate plumbing.

Thunderstorms were predicted and small craft warnings were posted. "Poppycock!" I pushed off from the wall and tried to recover my anchor. It was snagged. When I decided to cut it, it broke free. I slammed into the wall leaving the harbor. Things were going badly.

SNARED

A silver sun shone through the haze as we headed for Novi. The

INTO THE WALL

sun soon disappeared and it got dark, then darker. I couldn't imagine it getting darker but it did. Thunder rumbled in the west. There was no wind. Too late to turn back. Lightning cracked overhead. I took the sails down and sat in the bottom of the boat wrapped in the mainsail with my head outside. If the end was coming I wanted to see it.

7

STORM

A heavy rain pounded the seas flat. There still was no wind. I had meant to rig the boat up for heavy weather but never got around to it. I couldn't believe how dark it got. Lightning began flashing all about. The thunder was deafening. All that was missing was Mozart's "Requiem."

"I think very shortly you're going to be walking the dog," the boat said.

A sliver of light appeared on the horizon. It quickly expanded to the whole sky, and the sun came out. "You're being warned not to go to Novi," the boat told me.

"I think so," I acknowledged. We changed course for the Isles of Souls. The wind had come up and held steady at 12 knots. A fog set in. I wandered 20 degrees each side of the compass course. By noon I heard a foghorn and sailed for it.

HEADLAND

The horn got louder and higher. I could hear the roar of breakers.

The rocks came out of the fog quickly. I turned to the right, thinking of following them along, but there were rocks ahead. I turned again. The ocean dropped and a rock came out of the sea. "I must be on the coast," I said. But on the chart there was no horn along the coast. "Where the hell am I?" I kept shouting, while tacking and jibing to avoid the rocks. The fog lifted as quickly as the thunderstorm. High up on the rocks to my right was the Grand Hotel on Star Island, and to the left was the lighthouse. I was in the channel. "Great navigating!" I complimented myself.

MISTAKE SHOALS

"IDIOT"

"Idiot," the boat said.

We rounded the last buoy and sailed into the harbor. I picked up a mooring as far in as I could go, dropped the sails, and secured the boat. A woman in a pram passed close by. She was bringing her dog ashore so he could pump out his bilges. I asked for a lift and was rowed ashore with the dog.

DOG

There must have been fifty rocking chairs on the porch of the hotel, and they were all occupied by elderly people staring at me. An ancient came up to explain. "We couldn't believe anyone was out in that weather. After that awful storm and the fog. Then we saw your little sailboat." He looked at me trying to determine if I had a pact with the devil. He made me wish I'd been on the porch to see myself sailing out of the fog.

PORCH

I walked over the island to the church that the parishioners had burned down in olden times, then back to the dock to try to get a ride out to my boat. There was none to be had. The lifeguard called his supervisor on his radio. When this super-person came she told me that the island did not provide services to boaters. I felt that I had asked for a law of the cosmos to be altered. She did not like to set a precedent, but she would have to make an exception this one time since I was supposed to be off the island by sunset.

CHURCH

All the time I was being ferried to my boat I was scolded. I managed to ask if I could get breakfast in the morning. "Breakfast is only served to the guests of the

COSMIC LAW

10

hotel," I was told. Another cosmic law. I stood in my boat as she sped away and understood why the good people of the island had burned the church down.

Next morning I awoke at 0600 to a solar eclipse. I dared not go ashore, fearing the inhospitality of the natives during this phenomenon. From the boat I could see the prominent monument on the hill, dedicated three hundred years after the event so as not to be disputed, announcing that Captain John Smith made the only recorded visit to the islands in the spring of 1614. No one else had thought to bring a recorder. He stayed only a short time, trying desperately to teach the inhab-

SMITH

itants the new name of their islands, which he modestly named after himself. The natives stubbornly refused, referring to their island as the Isle of Holes. For consola-tion he declared himself Admiral of New England and sailed away to Smith-ologize the rest of the unknown world. Later, when the islands were taken over by fish-ermen, they managed to make an alcoholic brew from fish oil called shoals. From that day they were called the Isles of Shoals.

I bailed the ancient boat's nightly bladder failure and dis-covered a shroud was parting. Three stands were left. I lashed a line on it, not too securely, and then quickly forgot it. The wind had come up and strengthened enough to

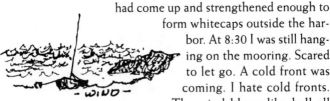

- WIND -

form whitecaps outside the har-bor. At 8:30 I was still hang-ing on the mooring. Scared to let go. A cold front was coming. I hate cold fronts. The wind blows like hell all day. I thought of staying another day, but I'd be stuck in a sta-tionary boat or else would have to go ashore and confront that superior person again. I thought about it a while, then put a double reef in the mainsail, plotted a course to Grouse Joint, thirty-five miles to the northeast 45 degrees, raised the sail, and cast off.

I sailed for buoy R24YL on my outdated chart, five miles away. The wind eased off and accommodatingly shifted so we could sail off the wind. Between Cape Feddick and Noon Island we accidentally jibed several times, which I am not supposed to admit to. I began rowing when the wind died and, as a reward for my good seamanship, the boom started banging me on the head until I lashed it properly.

OFF THE WIND

Moths and butterflies flew in from the sea and rested on the boat. The wind came out of the south again. Three flies appeared aboard. "Okay," I told the flies, "one of you will have to be killed to strike terror into you other two. Order has to be established by terror. It's worked for millions of years. No one likes it but that's the way it is." I rolled up a chart into a swatter. "Which of you will volunteer?"

ROWING

3 FLIES

"Did you ever consider that you have a slightly distorted view of life?" an audacious fly inquired.

"I've found my victim," I screamed angrily, swatting wildly. "Intelligence must go first to preserve order." The flies fled the ordered vessel.

Cape Purpose and Lecher's Neck passed to port. Across Waco Bay to Grouse Joint. The wind shifted and strengthened as we tacked for the high cliffs on shore. I grabbed a lobster buoy. It dragged, and we drifted towards the rocks. I cast off and sailed farther out where I grabbed another buoy and made a mess of a double-reefed mainsail. Luffing the jib and sailing on the main alone, we rounded the headland. I sailed to a club dock where two young attendants were puzzled by my request for a mooring.

"This is a very private club, and . . ." they were cut short by a profusely mustached older man.

"Take that one over there."

REEFING

"I'm beat and the bay is pretty bouncy. Is there a place I can stay the night?"

"Pull two cots together up in the club and sleep there. It's too expensive anywhere else."

After I had settled in he added, "Nobody will be here tonight; see you in the morning." And he left, never even asking me my name.

I walked a path along the cliffs and happened upon an old man seated on a stool sketching the sea. "Could you tell me where Winslow Homer's house is?"

HOMER

"It's up there," he pointed behind us. "Won't do you any good to go up there, though. Private property now. Can't get up there my-

PRIVATE

self. Property is more valuable than people now. Paintings are more valuable than the painters. Can't sell people anymore.

Art is merchandise now and the merchants don't even understand it, but they'll sell it. In the past we made icons that were worshipped; now we make collectibles for acquisitive people. Pictures are to look at, not to buy and sell. Looking is free. Seeing it, you don't have to own it."

He finished his sketch and signed it "W.H." "Don't mind my ravings, young man. Try to remain an idiotic optimist. It's healthier and more enjoyable."

MOGG

"Why didn't you sketch the tower?" I asked.

"It wasn't there when I was here. There's a dedication on it that says, 'To Chief Mogg, killed here in May of 1677.'"

"Why was he killed?" I asked.

"He was obstinate enough to think he had a perfect right to be here simply because his ancestors had been here for several thousand years. Don't mind me, young man. You'll come back grumbling platitudes after you're gone."

"I grumble platitudes now."

I left the old man chuckling to himself and returned to the club. Slept soundly. Woke at sunrise. Profuse Mustache had let himself in and made coffee. "Have a cup," he offered. "Goin' fishing. I'll motor you out to your boat."

The sea was flat calm with not a trace of a breeze. I rowed out of the harbor and headed for Richman's Island.

RICH·MAN'S ISLAND

LOG

I tried to go between the island and the mainland. The water shoaled and rocks appeared just beneath the surface. I backed off and went the proper way around the island. Off Cape Lizard we struck a floating log. Crossing Waco Bay we struck another log, reminding us that we were in logging country. Passing Brown How Now Island and Cape Smell, we sailed into See-Again's harbor. I dropped the anchor at the cable crossing sign and let the boat drift near the rocks. I leaped out with a stern line. "Well done," I complimented myself as the boat obediently drifted out.

ANOTHER LOG

SEE-AGAIN

I passed two carpenters merrily cursing their labors, "good morninged" them, and climbed the path to the lighthouse. Gulls were everywhere. The lightkeeper was painting a sign and, before I could say a word, he said, "Don't care how it looks, just so's it says what I want it to say."

SIGN

"It says just that," I said.

He took me up into the lighthouse. "Most of the time you can't see a damn thing—fog. But on a clear day you can see Mount Washington." Later he confided, "I love it here, could stay here the rest of my life. Me and the cat are the only two mammals on the island when you people leave."

I walked about the top of the island wondering how some people can be satisfied with so little. I returned to the beach to find the boat on the rocks. The rudder was protesting

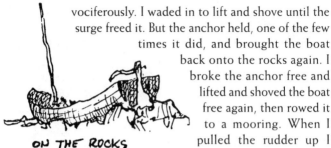

ON THE ROCKS

vociferously. I waded in to lift and shove until the surge freed it. But the anchor held, one of the few times it did, and brought the boat back onto the rocks again. I broke the anchor free and lifted and shoved the boat free again, then rowed it to a mooring. When I pulled the rudder up I found that the rudder track was broken. I went ashore again and asked one of the carpenters to drill two holes in the track so I could screw it back on.

"Sure," he said. He found the drill under a pile of tools. Then, luckily, he found a drill bit on the floor in a corner. I could tell he loved his work by the amount of time it took him to find things. He put the track on a metal grate and delicately positioned the bit in the track, then leaned his entire weight on the drill. I could tell he loved his tools truly because he was about to disembowel himself with one. When the drill bit punched through the track it spun the track around, grabbing his tee shirt and wrapping it up to his neck. "That's one done," he said, untangling himself.

CARPENTERS

I looked for blood. Amazingly, there was none. He put the drill on the track again. "Perhaps we should clamp it down," I suggested.

"Good thinking."

"And perhaps you should use a smaller drill to start the hole."

This was taken as interference and ignored. I returned to the boat with two holes in the track, grateful that I hadn't left a bloody mess on the island. I screwed on the track and slid on the rudder. It didn't go all the way down. The screw holes should have been countersunk. No way would I go back on that island to have that done. Half a rudder is better than no rudder at all.

A boat had come to take the carpenters ashore to the mainland. When they were all aboard, the motor wouldn't start. The mechanic hunched over it mumbling obscene incantations while the two carpenters complained, "Get that damn thing going, we can't stand this place. Don't want to spend another minute here. Get us off this island."

The motor went through its vocabulary of noises and then settled down to

MAROONED

a single sound. The boat shot out of the bay and made for the mainland at full throttle. I settled down to heating a can of beans. Cooking doesn't change the taste of beans, beans is beans . . . and crackers. I rigged the shelter and crawled into the sleeping bag. During the night a catboat came in and persistently circled us. I got up and asked if he wanted the mooring.

"Could we take it and you could hang off our stern?" he offered.

"Certainly," I replied in the best tradition of the sea. After the rearrangement was finished and all had retired, the boats started playing games bumping and circling one another. He and I

FOG

alternately fended the boats off throughout the night. Before sunrise I cast off and rowed away into the fog.

There was no wind that early in the morning, so I resignedly set the oars in the oarlocks and rowed through the fog for "My Rock N°2."

I never saw it. Found myself between Phantom Rock and

Stamma-store Island when the fog lifted briefly. We sailed between Lumpkin Island and Outer Huron without seeing them either. When the fog lifted, White Island was to port.

"This island is where Wright built a house," I explained to the boat. "Cut all the trees down to make an ugly little box on the very top of the rock. There he contentedly resides with a growing pile of trash beside it. Technology sends man into outer space while we live in ugly little wooden boxes. Wright's house represents the dangling end of the evolution of construction. Which has only been concerned with appearance. Could the house have generated its own power, reused its own refuse, been more self-contained, independent, less conspicuous? Doubtful. It stands atop the rock as an example of New England practically like an accumulation of bird droppings."

WRIGHT HOUSE

"Another profound statement from a do-nothing," the boat reminded me.

Strumpcaps Island to port. Crossing Horns Bay. Arriving at Crim-a-Lid River, avoiding the supernumerary lobster buoys. We sailed to the public dock against a fast outgoing tide. I should

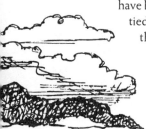

have botched it, but we came about smartly and tied up. Fishermen stood along the dock with their lines dangling idly in the water. The boat and I fell under the condemnation of these idlers.

"What the hell kind of a boat is that?" one asked.

"Look what he did to the hull," another said.

"Got to be crazy to sail outside a harbor in that."

"I think the green sails are pretty," a woman said, making matters worse.

"How's fishing?" I asked to change the subject.

"Nobody's caught a damn thing," one fisherman told me, "and nobody's had a bite all week."

"Why do you bother then?" I asked him.

"Part of our nature I guess. Can't help ourselves," he replied.

Fishing for survival has evolved into the art of doing nothing.

DOIN NOTHING

"Where can I get a mooring?" I asked the harbormaster.

"There are none," was the laconic answer. "Anchor up the river," he told me.

The river current had gotten stronger and the wind weaker, so we stayed tied to the dock for a few hours. I wandered about to find everything closed. The restaurant. The museum. Even the outdoor bathroom.

"The state of Maine is shut down," I was told, "because of lack of funds."

MAINE

In time the current eased up enough for us to row up river near the shore to a cove. We anchored in shallow water. The tide ebbed, leaving us on the mud. I couldn't get ashore because the mud was too deep. "Nothing ashore anyway," I told myself.

So I cooked beans and watched the terns fishing. Efficient little devils. Each time they dove they got a fish—they never missed. They were better fishermen than those triumphs of evolution on the dock with all their equipment.

The boat floated during the night. I awoke at sunrise and looked over the side. There was two feet of water to the bottom, so I went back to sleep. When I awoke again we were sitting on the mud. "You should have gotten into deeper water at sunrise, you donkey," the boat said. Now we had to wait for the return of the tide.

Luckily, the wind picked up when the tide refloated us. I cast

EBB

off at 9:00, and we slowly sailed the shore against the current. As we crossed Miss Congus Bay, a wasp came aboard. "Go forward where you belong," I commanded it. It stayed on my knee defiantly. "You know the penalty for refusing to obey an order at sea," I informed it. It ignored me. "Well, you're not going to ruin a good day by making me act objectionably," I said, and put him on a book and set him in the bow to act as lookout.

SEAL SPYING

A seal followed us. "You spying on us?" I asked.

"Just checking on what you're going to do."

"We're not going to do anything; we're just passing through."

"Everybody does something to foul up this area; then they complain that everything else is ruining it for them."

"We're just sailing through, complaining."

"Well, if you do, you're the exception." He continued following us like a cantankerous old wharfinger.

Old Harbor Sunken Ledge Buoy. Little Legg Rox. Eastern Legg Rox. Legg Rox North Ledge. Legg Rox South Ledge. Legg Rox Shoals. Larger boats stayed well offshore outside the navigational aids, while we could stay close to shore and enjoy the passing scenery.

LEGGS

This leads into praising the local boatbuilder. The Townie is built in Newbury, Massachusetts, not in China. It is a family-owned business, not an international conglomerate. You can actually speak directly to the builder, not to an assistant manager or a recording machine. The boat is designed to be sailed in these waters, not the Pacific, or the Caribbean, or the coasts of Europe. It's made of native woods, not imported exotic materials. The sails and parts can be gotten locally, not from California, Australia, or Japan. If damaged it can be easily repaired. It is a safe, comfortable boat and not a damn racing machine. It'll even talk to you if you take the time to listen.

Old Tramp Ledge. Wompson's Island. Save-Us Island.

Grinnen Island. Scupper Island. The low gray sky darkened to the north and northwest.

"How does that poem go?" I asked the boat. "Rain before wind . . . something happens; and wind before rain . . . something else happens?"

"I'm supposed to remember poems?" the boat complained. "Wait and see what the weather does." The weather held steady and didn't do anything, leaving me unenlightened.

I put on another pair of pants, another shirt, two sweaters and foul-weather gear, another hat, and a towel around my neck. I still couldn't conserve what little body heat I generated. I think as we grow older we start becoming cold-blooded animals.

PORT SLYDE

Entering Port Slyde, we tied up to the dock to the left of the main pier. I was told that there would be plenty of free moorings in this harbor. I found fifteen or twenty red buoys at ten dollars a night. Times were a-changing and Maine, when it wasn't shut down, was changing along with them. Ashore I walked around frantically trying to see something of interest. There was only an old fishing trawler converted to take passengers to Monhegan. So I sat among the local do-nothings and watched the boat take on and discharge its daily catch of tourists.

We anchored and in the morning breakfasted with the other migrants at the old Ocean Hotel. From the window I could see a tree house kids had built. The tree should have been

OCEAN HOTEL

more considerate and grown into a house instead of a silly tree. We cleared the harbor by 8:00 A.M., sailing between Mosquito Head and Mosquito Island and rounding One, Two, and Three Bush Islands. Eleven sportfishing boats raced by headed south. Hunting. All wild things are hunted: the fish, the fowl, the animals of the forests. Trapped, shot, and poisoned, for fun and profit; pursued every moment of their miserable lives. There's a price tag on every living thing, and if it can't be killed for profit then it's killed for the sheer joy of it. As if we were given divine instructions to kill every damn living thing we can.

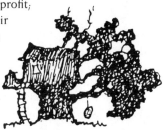

TREE HOUSE

11 SPORTSMEN HUNTING

"Does that say something about you?" the boat asked. I couldn't reply and wondered if we had even one redeeming quality. Intelligence?

The wind lightened. Other sailboats closer to the land seemed to be moving better. I remembered that the sun heats up the land and the air rises above it and the colder sea air rushes in to fill the void, creating a sea breeze near the land. We should have stayed closer to shore.

23

We crossed the West Wenobshott, passing Little Green Island, Large, Larger, Great, Greater, Greatest, etc., Green Islands. Ought-To Island. Brimstone, Saddleback, Brandies. Three of the eleven sportsfishermen returned, speeding by. Caught what they wanted

RETURNING

and had to get back. Forever in a hurry. Can't go fast enough. I thought of going into Venalhaven, but the weather held steady with plenty of light left so we continued on to Moore's Ledge, Wreck Rock, Harbor Point Head.

Things changed. The wind headed us. We were forced to tack against an outgoing tide. I should have waited for the tide to change, but that would have been too reasonable. So we sailed and rowed and grumbled until we approached the public dock on the Isle of Woe. It was crowded with people fishing.

"Can't they do nothing somewhere else?" I asked, suddenly becoming aware of how outlandishly over-decorated the boat looked. "I'm embarrassed," I explained to the boat.

"You're embarrassed!" the boat screamed at me. "You let your silly instincts run amuck, and then I have to live with the results."

"We'll sail by. I don't want to have to explain you to those people on the dock."

"A fine state of affairs. I'd like to explain *you* to them," the boat replied. As we sailed by, the fishermen's heads turned and then their mouths dropped open. They pulled their lines in and left. They had lost their concentration, and fishing for nothing takes concentration.

I spotted a private dock a short distance away. We tacked for it and hit bottom. I pulled the centerboard up a little and continued heading for it. We grounded out completely at the dock with the centerboard up and the rudder out. If the weather got bad we'd be pounded to pieces on the rocky bottom. The situation got worse. The boom and sail snarled on the pilings, and the wind pinned us to the dock. I dropped the sails and rowed off, only to run up on more rocks. A sight-seeing boat with gawking passengers passed us. The captain's head popped out of the pilothouse window, explaining us away as an example of poor navigation. The boat and I swore and argued at one another until the wake of the sight-seeing boat freed us. Now the boat wouldn't head into the wind when I rowed, so I let the bow fall off completely and rowed the damn thing backwards.

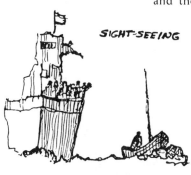

SIGHT-SEEING

Only one fisherman remained at the dock to greet us. "Never saw a sailboat rowed backwards," he said.

"Sails forward, rows backward," I explained. "How's fishing?" I asked, to keep communication alive.

BACKWARDS

"Not catching a damn thing," he replied, as I expected.

"Anything of interest to see on the island?" I asked.

"If you go up that road and turn right there's nothing to see for miles. But if you go to the left there's the church, post office, town hall, court, store, and library." He pointed

STONE HOUSE

out a mooring I could hang on for the night. I walked up to the road and turned left. In a short time I came upon a small stone building that housed church, post office, town hall, court, store, and library. It was closed.

The rest of the time I watched a crow in a treetop. I doubt if he realized how important he was at that moment. He was observed and thought about, the focus of attention to the exclusion of everything else. What a distortion of reality. I'm sure if he had been aware of the attention he was getting he would have hammed it up with a few jokes and a little soft-shoe. Crows are like that.

I returned to the boat and rowed out to the mooring. Two schooners soon came in and dropped anchor, rowing

CROW

SCHOONER

their passengers ashore so they could stare in wonder at the island's small, efficient stone building.

A good night's sleep and oatmeal in the morning sent us on our way to Yawns Island.

We sailed by Blake Island and continued through Burnt Island Thorofare and around the northern end of the Isle of

Woe. Between Bookend Point and another Burnt Island. Then Grog Island, Grite Ledge and Green Rock, leaving Martial Island to port. Popplerpope, Pallow Ledge, Perron Island, Primstone Island, Parbar Island, Mooseberry Island, and on to Mockamock Head into an ebbing tide, rounding the lighthouse at Burnt Toast Harbor to the little town of Swains.

We tied up at a dock and asked a local if there was anything of interest to see on the island.

"Walk to the lighthouse. Only thing to do around here," he suggested despairingly.

ISLE OF WOE LIGHT

So I walked to the lighthouse. There was a museum inside with tools and photographs of the good old days when granite was quarried on the island. There were long group photographs of the men who worked the stone. All dressed in the same short jackets, heavy pants, and soft hats—hundreds of men in prison garb to cut stone. There were stories of the rotten work conditions, injuries and deaths from the machinery, weather, and stone dust. I wondered what happened to all those men. Probably went off and did some other ridiculous thing that some predatory entrepreneur thought society wanted done. So much for social planning. There was none then and very little now.

STONE CUTTERS

I found myself walking to the lighthouse several times to stare at the photographs and marvel at the sorcery of the economics we survive in. All roads on the island led to that dismal past. To escape my dismal state of mind I bushwhacked across the island until I didn't know where I was. I tranquilly stumbled through the wilderness and broke out onto a golf course. "Keep Out, Private, Players Only!" the sign screamed at me.

"I could stumble through a rain forest for days and not be surprised to stumble out onto a goddamn golf course," I told the smug sign. I sat in the shade and tried to remember what I knew of the game of Golf.

It was known to have been played by the Romans in 43 A.D. and called "Pagania," meaning "game of nonsense." It was rediscovered by St. Andrew in Scotland in the fourteenth century, named by the Dutch "kolf," meaning to strike an object with a scepter, and developed by the English, who declared it by proclamation to be the "Royal Game." Peasants and common folk were forbidden to play. Later it was adopted by the Americans and played by them more than any other sport, because, of course, it was the "Royal Game," and it is well known that all American golfers are descended from royalty.

ROYAL GAME

In the fifteenth century it was banned entirely for interfering with the sport of archery, which was needed for warfare— another "Royal Game" Americans have adopted. Wars are declared on their golf courses or on fishing trips.

An eighteen-hole golf course requires twenty-five acres, tons of chemical fertilizer, pesticides, and animal repellents that render the entire surroundings so sterile and repugnant to life-forms that only special grasses and golfers can tolerate it. The ball cannot be more than 1.62 ounces in weight and not larger than 1.67 inches in diameter for reasons unknown to every-

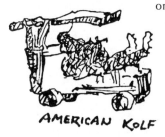

AMERICAN KOLF

one. In the beginning, players ran over the course, the object being to play as quickly as possible. Later they walked. Now they ride and take as long as they possibly can to finish a "round" of that most ancient of "Royal Games of Nonsense."

When I returned, the boat said, "Can't you go ashore as a simple, kindly tourist and not as a marauding berserker? You've savaged every little coastal town we've landed at. Then you merrily sail away toward another defenseless town."

I mumbled a reply.

"What? What? Speak up," the boat insisted.

I mumbled again, having no rebuttal. I crawled into the sleeping bag and went to sleep. It was the only thing to do with an argumentative boat.

I awoke at 5:00 and sailed out of the harbor while it was still dark. It is a wonderful feeling to sail out of a harbor, alone in the darkness with nobody else about, knowing the light will gradually come with the whole day before us. Perhaps it's just the leaving the harbor that makes me feel so good. Schools of small fish occasionally ruffled the water, giving me a feeling of comradeship. Gulls obligingly told me how close I was to the inhospitable shore.

STILL DARK

Barbar Island, Baker Island, Blister Island, Black Island, Little Gott Island, and Great Gott Island led up into the Western Way to Southwest Harbor. I intended to stay there for the night but it was too early and a brisk following wind was too inviting, so we continued on up into Gnomes Fiord. I had been warned that if we hit the tide wrong in this place we would be sailing backward. Not knowing the stage of the tide simplified matters. "Not to worry," I told the boat, "we'll contend with it when we get there."

Gnomes Fiord was great sailing. It was five miles to Gnomes Harbor. The tide appeared to be with us. Many larger boats were coming down on us against the tide and wind, so their planning was not as good as our non-planning. "Wait for it to overwhelm you and then be damned," the boat said cynically.

We ended up sailing into the small harbor

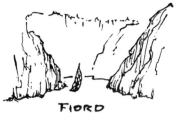

FIORD

at Gnomes Village. This was a perfect little harbor, new dock and pier. The anchorage was good and not crowded. There were few people. But something was wrong. Something was there, or wasn't there, that drove me away.

"The only reason you don't like this village is because you can't find anything to verbally savage," the boat reminded me.

I didn't reply to its unassailable logic but just accepted it as another humiliating flogging while hurriedly casting off to sail back down the fiord. The wind was gusting now as we beat into it. We luffed up many times to let gusts pass and hugged the shore trying to keep out of the stronger gusts. As darkness came on we sailed into Southwest Harbor. It looked like a high-priced car lot. Sleek black hulls, nothing under 35 feet, moored row after row after row. Toys that no one could afford anymore. Makes you wonder.

CARLOT

I had a hard time finding the town. I didn't know where it was. When I did find it we were forced to sail up and down before the floats. The only float with open space was used by the Coast Guard; I was promptly and officially kicked off. The wind was still strong. We jibed and came about many times before I could ask a fisherman how the anchoring was. "Bad. Take that mooring beside you, it's my spare."

The town I grudgingly compliment, but not so far as to where I can apply a definitive adjective. Enough said.

We sailed in the morning for Stonington. A large Friendship sloop played leapfrog with us. When the wind blew they passed us, but when it lightened up we passed them. It was a hot, cloudless day with predominantly light airs. We passed Egg Rock; how many Egg Rocks are there? Long Ledge, Lazy Gut Island, Lamb Island, Log Island, into the Leer Island Thorofare and its multitude of islands, amongst which we could play, where larger boats stayed timidly away. Hurray for a small boat in which you feel the freedom of a fish and the affinity of the sea.

We tacked to the Stonington dock in almost dead air. "You

must be the *Damn Foole*," the boat was greeted. "There's no other boat in the world like you." A woman was complimenting the boat, completely ignoring me. I was used to that. I had a dog that everyone loved while everyone hated me. It upset me for a while until I read a scientific paper that said that it was suspected that genes jump species. You can be near someone or something and genes will jump back and forth like fleas. So I believed that the dog stole all my genes and gave me his; then the boat stole all the dog's genes from me and left me with the personality of an old wooden boat. That's why I am ignored and disliked. I left the woman and the boat talking with one another and went into the town. When I returned I asked the boat if it had discussed me.

"No, you're not worth talking about." We sailed out into the dark to find a mooring.

In the morning we sailed out through a fog set into Penobscot Bay. Midway across I spied a large ship off to starboard headed for us. It stayed in the same relative position to us, which meant that we were on a collision course. I should go behind it. I watched its bow. There didn't appear to be a bow wave. It wasn't underway. The ugly, rusty ship sitting stationary there was a puzzlement. There was no name on the bow and no flags to identify it. We crossed its bow and sailed on into the fog. The light at Rockport Harbor soon appeared. We rounded it and sailed for the public dock.

There I met the harbormaster and asked him

TO THE PUBLIC DOCK —

about that ship. He told me it was a Russian fish factory ship and that it had been given permission by the governor of Maine to fish in the bay. "Incredible isn't it? I used to fish," the harbormaster said, "but now you can't make a living at it anymore. One time not too long ago anyone could come down to the shore and drop a line into the water and

PILLAGE AND PLUNDER SHIP

catch a fish. There's no fish now. Then our governor tells the Russians to come over and plunder what's left.

Rockport is listed in the National Register of Historic places. Once kilns here converted limestone into lime which was used to make mortar and finish plaster. In the nineteenth century, Rockport was a major supplier of lime. There were fifteen local quarries. Wood was supplied for the fires in the kilns. They burned day and night. Can you imagine working in the quarries or at the kilns or even on a schooner delivering the lime to New York and all the towns on the East Coast? The deadening, backbreaking, mankilling slavery?

LIME

The advent of cement and a disastrous fire in 1907 put a merciful end to it. This is the last surviving evidence of Rockport's industrial past. Do we want to remember it? I'm sure there are a lot of people who don't. In time every place will have a plaque commemorating an unforgettable historical event.

Now Rockport is a tourist and retirement community. It was celebrating its centennial. A photography shop displayed its wares and lectured on its craft. "Is photography art?" they

ROCKPORT

asked. "Is art art?" they should have asked. It's all merchandise now. They're living in the dark age of culture trying to define culture.

In the morning there was thunder but no rain. Sailing out of the harbor I went forward to attach the jib leads. The boat turned off suddenly and headed for the biggest boat in the harbor, going like hell, with intentions of destroying it. I abandoned the jib and stumbled back to the tiller, jibing in time to just come within a hair's breadth of that virgin glass.

"Bad boat! At the mooring you come about, jibe, reach and beat impatiently. But when I sail to a mooring or a dock you don't quite make it, or sail backwards. Half the time I don't know what this goddamn boat is going to do!"

"Bad owner, bad boat."

"Bull."

Camden was just a short sail away. We charged into its crowded harbor, wing and wing, like a bird of prey coming into a rookery. We got that look of disbelief from all those sitting comfortably on their spacious pleasure boats. The channel was narrow and winding. Jibing several times, we had to go to the very end of the harbor to the public

CAMDEN

dock behind the schooners. We tied up with the prams.

I left the boat and walked into the town to make a phone call. I called Ken and asked him to meet me in Rockport to haul the boat out. The vacation was over. He suggested we could haul out at Rockland or Rockport. He's a Gemini and can't make a decision, and always complicates matters by giving himself alternatives. I'm a Taurus. I make a decision and can't change it. So a Taurus was trying to make an appointment with a Gemini. We agreed that we'd meet at either of the two harbors the next day before noon.

GEMINI   TAURUS

When I returned to the boat I found I had been ticketed. A bright red ticket hung from a shroud telling me I was in violation of some maritime law and to report to town hall for punishment. We cast off and raced equally fast out of the harbor, tied up to a vacant mooring and spent the night.

Next day we sailed for the two harbors. We ran freely before a strong wind pushed by an equally strong tide. I was a little concerned about the boat holding together, but hell, this was the last day, let 'er rip!

We passed a beach where legend says that two warring tribes faced each other one autumn day in the distant past. In full battle regalia, painted and feathered as ferociously as could be imagined, holding their diabolically ingenious weapons in nervous hands, they shouted threats and insults across the open space between the lines. Threats turned to jokes and then questions. The chiefs were up on higher ground arranging the conditions for battle. The sun rolled slowly up in the sky.

A ball floated in from the sea and rolled up on the sand between the two confrontational tribes. It stopped midway between them. A southerly wind blew it towards the northern line.

BALL

A northern warrior, thinking it came from the southern tribe, gave the ball an angry kick back. A southern warrior, seeing it coming from the north, gave the ball an angry kick in return. The ball went back and forth several times until a southern warrior broke from his tribe and ran kicking the ball across the sand trying to kick it through the northern line. The northerner who stopped the ball ran kicking it towards the southern line chased by the southerner. Now two southerners intercepted it and passed it between themselves towards the north. Northerners came to meet them. More and more warriors dropped their weapons and ran out to kick the ball. The chiefs were angry when they saw what was happening and tried to stop it. But they could not. It was not to be a serious day. The game ended at sunset.

Exhausted, the warriors swam in the ocean and were

reunited with their families. They gathered clams and fish and other foods that were abundant along the shore and feasted into the night celebrating the ball game. The ball was greater than their councils, greater than their chiefs, greater than their holy men. The ball had spoken to them. It happily showed them how to avoid what they did not want to do. The beach was called "The place where the ball told us we could not fight."

I felt I had gone too far. Sailing far offshore we missed Rockport and Rockland completely. How can anyone miss two harbors? We did. We sailed over to a lobsterman. "Where is Rockland?" I asked.

"What?" he questioned in answer to my question.

"Where is Rockland?"

"What?"

We exchanged questions until he shut his engine off. He couldn't hear a thunderclap with it going. In fact, I think all lobstermen are as deaf as dead herring from listening to their engines.

"Where's Rockland?"

"Back that way about three miles."

The wind died and the tide strengthened. I rowed cussing and perspiring profusely. It was late. I was expected at the ramp at 12:00. We rounded Howl's Head at 1:00 and made Rockland ramp by 2:00. I tied up and took the boom off. When I unfastened the shrouds the mast broke and collapsed, falling to port between two powerboats.

"Is that the way you take the mast down?" I was asked by their owners.

"That's the way this mast comes down," I replied,

MAST —

disregarding the stares that accused me of being a lunatic. The mast had broken before and now had broken at one of its many splices. I had a strange feeling it would break. It must have been as tired as I was.

Ken arrived an hour later. He had gotten lost. He had too many decisions to make and was halfway to Canada before he stopped making them. The boat was put on the trailer, and we started back for me to continue my dull, disgruntled life.

"Don't drive too fast," I told Ken.

"Stop telling me what to do," he replied, and then added, "I know a shortcut." He drove off in a rush to get lost.

The Townie and the Damn Foole

I awoke at 5:00 A.M. "Good morning," my best half greeted me.

"Bullshit," my worst half replied.

"Am I going to have to put up with you all day?" the best half asked the worst half.

GOOD MORNING

"Everyone else has to put up with me," the worst replied.

"Well, I'm not going to, not today, and I'm not doing what you tell me to do."

"You do the same thing every day," the worst half sneered.

"Not today, I'm going sailing."

"You can't, you'll be fired. You've got bills to pay. People rely on you. The work you do will never get done."

"Bullshit," the best half repeated the worst half's original response to the morning. "And you stay here," the good half continued.

"What?" the worst half screamed.

"You stay home," the best half commanded, "I don't want you in my boat."

On the way out I slammed the door and locked it. "Well, I may be only half here," I said to myself, "but I've got the best half today."

I breakfasted at a little diner and then phoned work. They accepted my excuse matter-of-factly. "That's how essential you are in this grand scheme of things," I chuckled.

LOCKED IT IN

BREAKFASTED

Soon I was carrying my sailbag through the ancient hallowed halls of the Corinthian Yacht Club of Marblehead. I had sailed the Townie up a few days earlier for the coming Race Week. Now I had the chance to sail along the shores of a harbor other than Nahant. There was no one about, so I sat on the spacious porch and waited. I could see the Townie languidly swinging on its mooring in the sleepy little harbor. "It's going to be a great day," I told the sky. "No fooling around."

SAILBAG

"We can't promise you that, can we?" the sky asked the ocean.

"You take your chances like everyone else," the ocean told me.

"Just keep it within reason," I said less demandingly. The sky and the ocean laughed at me. Then a busy young girl happened by.

"Can I get a ride out to my boat?" I asked.

"You'll have to wait until I fire the cannon and raise the flag," she said as she dashed off to do just that, along with everything else that had to be done. I remained sitting on the deserted porch watching the motionlessness of the view. There were no birds or clouds. The sun hung stolidly in place. The boats dared not move. Suddenly the cannon fired and the flag shot up the pole. The startled chair threw me over backwards. Clouds appeared. Birds, bugs, and butterflies flew. The sun began climbing and everything moved that was supposed to move. And the other poor things that couldn't, tried.

"Ready?" the busy girl bellowed. I hurriedly collected my sailbag and followed her obediently down the ramp to the launch. The motor roared. "Which one?" she demanded.

"The little green Townie by the rocks," I timidly

42

answered. We rushed off towards it, jostling the other boats with our wake. We came alongside. I stepped aboard.

"Cute little boat you have," the busy girl said as she sped off, leaving us bouncing in the turbulence she seemed so fond of creating.

"Good morning," the boat said. "I thought you'd turn up here today."

"I didn't know myself until this morning, when my worst half started giving me a bad time."

"You didn't bring it with you, did you?"

CUTE LITTLE BOAT

"No, I locked it up."

"Good, that half is hard to take," the boat said.

I purposefully went about preparing the boat slowly, enjoying the simple ageless tasks, savoring the anticipated elation that the boat and I would experience when I cast off. First I bailed out the water that had come in overnight. Then I hanked the jib onto the forestay and tied the tack to the stemhead with a short line, reminding myself that I should buy a proper fitting. When I pulled the ancient mainsail out of the bag, I chided myself for not having folded it. I slid the foot onto the boom and the luff up the mast, slipped the broken battens into the torn pockets, put the rudder on the transom, popped the tiller into it, and lashed it amidships. I lowered the centerboard, then sat back and watched the telltale lifting, indicating the beginning of a southwest

AGELESS TASK

wind. "That must be the last task for that busy little girl," I told the boat. "Are we ready?"

"We're ready," the boat replied jubilantly.

I raised the jib, then the main, tightened the halyards and outhaul, then went forward and cast off the mooring line, back-winding the jib so the bow would fall off the wind and turn towards the open sea. A mystical content-ment settled over the boat as it slid through the water on the ebbing tide. We wove through all the grand yachts in that crowded harbor, greeting them by name and port of call. They re-sponded glumly.

TOWARD THE OPEN SEA

"We must be the smallest, cheapest, and least seaworthy, but we're the only ves-sel sailing out to enjoy this fine day. To be at the whim of the wind and the sea, alone in a small boat on a perfect day, is an experience not to be exceeded."

An expensive racing machine laughed at us derisively. We sailed close by and threw a bucket of bilge water into its per-fectly dry cockpit. It fumed and sputtered, draining it out an-grily. When we were clear of the harbor I set the jib out opposite the main with a whisker pole and raised the cen-terboard. We ran grace-fully before the wind over the long ocean swells. The horizon was lost in the haze while the

BILGE WATER

sun was too bright to look at. The sky was clear. The little girl was probably too busy and had overlooked the clouds.

We sailed between Eagle Island and its spindle. Beyond we closed with Baker's Island. I decided to visit its lighthouse. We sailed to the wharf to find that there was no dock or ladder, only an unfriendly sign reading, "Private, No Trespassing," with an added warning to beware of guard dogs. Another sign should have been there facing into the island reading, "Owners Are Not Permitted to Leave Their Private Property. You Are to Remain on This Island for the Duration of Your Ownership."

We jibed away and made for the Misery Islands off the shores of Pride's Crossing. When we arrived I drove the boat up on the beach of Great Misery on the run. The sails held it on shore as I ran the anchor line up the beach to a stout piece of driftwood. The boat banged around a while on the rocky beach until the tide receded and left it alone. The island was mine! I took off my shoes and perched them on a prominent rock, officially taking possession. "I'm going to explore the island," I told the boat.

"To find plunder and slaves," the boat added.

BEACHED

MINE

"Of course I'll Christianize the poor devils, and the plunder will be used to advance civilization." I marched

MARCHED INLAND

inland over the rocks and rolling hills, through the groves of trees and past the dense underbrush. "Everything here is mine," I kept reminding myself greedily. The birds sang cheerfully. The flowers breathed their fragrances. The vegetation reflected the sun's heat. I was ignored and left to ponder why it was called Misery Island.

I returned to the boat and was immediately asked, "Where's the plunder? Where are the slaves?"

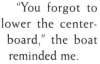

WHERE'S THE PLUNDER

"There aren't any," I told the boat. "All the slaves have gone ashore long ago into the towns to sell the plunder in the stores and specialty shops."

"You're a fine example of humanity, can't even pillage and plunder properly," the boat said. "Let's get afloat, it's too fine a day to spend on land."

I recovered the anchor line and pushed the boat over the rocks back into the water. When I sheeted in the sails we started drifting towards some rocks.

"You forgot to lower the centerboard," the boat reminded me.

I released the

lanyard, but the board wouldn't descend. The rocks drew closer. I jammed a screwdriver down the hole on top of the trunk and pounded on the board with an oar. Rocks tumbled out and the board slid down. We sailed away from my kingdom that had almost plundered and enslaved me. Manchester was ahead. I had never been into that harbor because its long winding channel made it difficult to sail into and

WITH AN OAR

AWAY ————

out of. The wind had swung around to the east coming over the starboard beam—an ideal wind to reach into and out of the channel. We sailed by the entrance buoy, and the wind lightened, interrupted by the land. We slowly glided past the moored boats into the inner harbor. New, large, showy toys on strings, sadly idle, waited patiently for the children to come out and play. We found the public docks at the very end of the

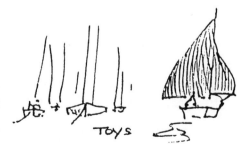

TOYS

channel and tied up. There were no other boats there. I lowered the sails and walked through the park into town. I walked the streets with my senses turned off, my nervous system short circuited.

INTO TOWN

I recovered when I returned to the boat, raised the sails, and cast off. On the way back out to the open sea we sailed through a fleet of Dyer Dhows raced by laughing children. Outside we stayed close in to shore and played among the rocks. A small boat is great for getting into trouble. The rocks adroitly dodged us as the wind freshened. We sailed on over into Salem Harbor and across the flats, avoiding the channel. I kept looking over the side expecting the bottom to suddenly rise up and grab us. But it must have been the right time of tide.

DYER DHOWS

ROCKS

We sailed uninterruptedly to Derby Wharf. I tied up on an old pier and walked ashore

DERBY WHARF

to read the sign that faced into the town. "Do Not Use This Pier," it read.

"I've already used it. It's a sailing boat. That should be considered when I'm brought to trial." I sat in the sun and thought of the bygone witch trials here, the East Indies shipping, the cursed judge in the House of Seven Gables, and of Hawthorne watching Salem Harbor from the window of the Custom House.

7 GABLES

The wind was still building, and the sky was now changing rapidly when I returned to the boat, so I put a reef in the mainsail before raising it. I cast off and sailed for the far shore, Marblehead's West Shore. The wind was too

REEFED

strong, and the sail was a mess, with large folds coming off the boom. When I reached the lee of the shore I grabbed a lobster buoy, pulled down the main, and then bent on and raised the "chicken sail."

The sky darkened in the west and

STORM COMING

thunder rumbled periodically. We sailed along close in to shore hiding from the rising wind and chop. We passed close by Fort Sewall. We were doing hull speed now. A jogger ran past us high up on the wall. "Must be one of those super athletes," I explained to the boat. Then a woman casually walking a dog passed us. I offered no excuse for this to the boat as we thrashed and pounded through the water at top speed. Then an old man shuffled by us dragging a cane.

I hiked out and sheeted in to try to stay with him, but he inched ahead of us. We passed him only after he collapsed on a bench and stared pensively at his toes, completely ignoring our victory.

Now we were at the harbor entrance, exposed to the full fury of the wind. "Should take the jib off," the boat advised.

"If I do I won't be able to point," I explained, luffing the jib. I felt the first drops of rain. "When it rains, it'll rain hard, and there won't be any visibility. We'll be in trouble," I reminded the boat.

"Sail well beyond the mooring and then tack to make sure we make it," the boat told me. The sky was black when we tacked and looked as though it should have been raining well before then. When we came into

RAIN

the wind, the boat came to a dead stop as its bow bumped the mooring. I tied up quickly and dropped the sails over us as the rain came down heavily. The boat and I laughed uncontrollably, realizing that it couldn't have been timed better.

When the rain let up I straightened up the boat and gave two blasts on the horn. Soon the little girl came out in the motor launch. "I watched you sail in before it rained. You should have called and I would have come out and got you," she scolded.

SHOULD HAVE CALLED

"I didn't want to inconvenience anyone," I explained, and got an angry stare. "I like the rain," I added, trying to wiggle out of the guilt of depriving her of running the world. Ashore, I sat back on the porch and watched the sun fall out of the sky in obedience to the cannon and the flag lowering. The world stood still once more. It couldn't have been a better day . . . in a Townie.

ON THE PORCH AGAIN

Maine
Again

I had to sail somewhere. Anywhere. The wind had been blowing 30 knots for three days with intermittent rain. "The weather should clear now," I told myself. Vacation time gave me seven desperate days to purge myself of the tedium of "making a living." I stood on the dock with sixty dollars worth of food, ten trashbags of clothes and equipment, along with water jugs, anchor, oars, life jacket, lantern, etc.

EQUIPMENT

I had one thing to do before I started. I climbed a ladder to the Dory Club roof, pulling up a short ladder which I leaned against the new cupola. Then I got the windvane I had made and set it on the copper dome, lined it up carefully with the north, sealed it in place with roofing cement, and

CLUB ROOF

secured it with lagbolts. "That's done," I told myself as I put
the ladders and tools away. "Now I can go sailing."

I grabbed somebody's oars from the
Club and threw somebody's pram
into the water and rowed out
to the Townie. "I was expecting you," the boat said.

"Well, you know more
than I do."

SOMEBODY'S
PRAM AND OARS

"That's not too difficult," the boat
replied. "Where are we going?"

"Maine again," I answered, and cast off the mooring line. I
rowed the boat to the dock, squeezing in
between powerboats and lobster boats

SQUEEZED IN

that seem to be permanently tied up there. Then I portaged all the equipment to the boat, including a small cuddy that I bolted to the coaming. It would give me shelter and a place to hide when I got scared. Much better than putting a bucket over my head.

When I returned with the last load, a figure stood at the end of the wharf. I'd have to walk around it. Damn it, I knew what it was. "Where are you going?" it would ask.

"Sailing," I'd reply.

"You know what the tide's doing?" it would ask.

"Don't care what the tide's doing," I'd answer.

"Don't have a watch either, do you?"

IT STOOD THERE

"Don't want one."

"You know what day this is?" It was Friday, traditionally a bad day to sail.

DAMN WEATHERVANE

"I don't give a damn what day this is. Get out of my way!"

It stepped aside. "Your windvane is backwards, you damn fool."

"Oh, no," I say to myself in despair, ignoring it, trying to not show my vulnerability. I threw the last bag aboard and cast off. Ran out the oars and rowed out to clear water.

There was no wind. I looked back at the windvane on the cupola. East was west and north was south. "Did you see me putting that weathervane up backwards?" I asked the boat.

"Certainly," the boat replied.

"You saw me making that mistake and never said a word?" I asked.

"I never interfere with mistakes that are beneficial."

"How so?"

"Mistakes delight the Great Spirit, and it usually rewards those responsible. Your blundering guarantees us good weather."

"I don't want to hear any more of your primitive paganism," I said, exasperated. "That damn weathervane can stay that way forever." I lowered the centerboard, slid the rudder and tiller into place, bent on the mainsail, put in the battens, and raised it. Then I hanked the jib onto the forestay and raised it, backwinding it. The wind appeared just enough to push the bow to leeward. I stepped back into the cockpit and took the helm. This was the only time I sincerely felt good: when I sailed out of a harbor, escaping from all my mistakes. It was my supreme moment.

ESCAPING

We reached through Shag Rocks, then ran before a typically gentle southerly wind for Gloucester. I pulled out the charts, spilling coffee on them, cussing the crowded boat. "I've got to get a bigger boat."

The boat laughed. "You're repeating what every boat owner says every day. Forget it."

CHARTS

I had put my toothbrush in a conspicuous place; from then on it hid from me for the rest of the voyage. Expect one item to do this, and if you try to find it, it will drive you crazy. Forget it.

Passing close to a lobsterboat, I shouted, "Good morning." The lobsterman heard me but didn't reply. "Nice day," I continued. No reply. A dog on board barked. I barked back. "I'd rather talk to your dog anyway," I shouted, and barked a few more times.

BARK   BARK

It was a clear day. I found myself at the starting line of the outer Brimbles. Marbleheaders in their racing craft were swarming all about us. A shot was fired, indicating five minutes to the start of the race. The sailing became frenzied. "Bang," went the start. I tacked to port to get out of the way of their starboard start. Another class of boats approached the line, to be sent off in turn, while other boats awaited their turns. Each would sail the same triangular course. The objective, of course, was to sail the triangle better than everyone else. "Good luck, triangular sailors," I saluted them, recalling my own futile efforts at this bemusement.

START   Sixty degrees magnetic north brought us inside Halfway Rock. Seabirds sat atop it, whitening the rock with their droppings. I imagine they are reminded daily, in a very British manner, that "Everyone is expected to do his duty, and those who don't can leave, there's no room for malingerers." Another leisurely pastime takes on the chores of a duty.

We sailed past Norman's Woe and Hammond Castle. Then a large platform structure appeared out-

DUTY ON HALFWAY ROCK

side Gloucester Harbor. "What the hell is that?" I asked the boat.

"You got me," the boat replied.

I imagine most people in the town don't even know what it is. It must have appeared on the water suddenly, an alien growth that will forever remain a mystery.

It was still early afternoon and the wind was steady, so we avoided Gloucester Harbor, which is full of private yacht clubs on one side and

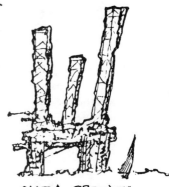

ALIEN GROWTH

commercial fishing piers on the other. With no public ramp in the harbor, you grab a mooring and there's no way to get ashore. You bounce in the wakes of boats late at night and early in the morning. As you can guess, I don't care for Gloucester Harbor and I'd just as soon avoid it.

We continued around Cape Ann, sailing close to the Coast Guard Station with a good wind and a favorable tide.

CAPE ANN

57

Then inside Milk Island and Thatcher's twin lights. The sun was bright and hot, so I popped open an umbrella and sat in the shade while running for Straitsmouth Island. The wind shifted several times, making us jibe to stay on course until we rounded Halibut Point.

TWIN LIGHTS

OUT OF THE SUN

Now we were on a reach and could feel the true force of the wind. We hid from the gusts by staying close to shore. The hole in the wall leading into Lanesville came abeam. The land blanketed the wind, so I dropped the main and jib and ran out the oars, rowing into the narrow entrance. A man stood on the wall, watching us struggle against the outgoing tide that eventually slammed us against the wall at his feet. I threw him a line. Without a word being

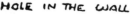

HOLE IN THE WALL

WALL

said, he caught it and lined us through the gut. I dropped an anchor off the stern while he tied the bow line to a ring on the top of the wall. Then he waved and walked on.

I climbed ashore and joined the birds and people on top of the wall to

SUNSET

watch the sun drop into Ipswich Bay. It was a beautiful night with
a chill in the breeze that kept the bugs from being pesty. The stars
sparkled around a full moon. I lay
awake in the sleeping bag beyond midnight, enjoy-
ing where I was.

NIGHT

Next morning I awoke to the wakes and drones of the motors
of outgoing lobsterboats. I dressed, looked for the toothbrush,
then went ashore to breakfast at the local restaurant. Breakfast
takes me through the day. Returning to the boat, I climbed the
wall facing the ocean to see the wind on the water. It was strong
for that early in the day. There were whitecaps, and whitecaps
scare me when I'm ashore considering my small open boat.

To alleviate my fears, I put a reef in the mainsail before
I raised it. I cast off from the wall, recovered my anchor, and rowed out
the mouth of the harbor. The
northeast wind kept us
close hauled for Halibut
Point. The boat was heading

HALIBUT POINT

for Nova Scotia. "I'd like to go there," I told the boat.

"See what the wind does," the boat said. Soon the wind dropped and I shook out the reef, and shortly the wind disappeared. It was typical of the area. We were at the bell off Halibut Point. "We'll just have to wait and see where the wind wants us to go," the boat said.

"The hell with going anywhere! I just sailed away from there. I'm in no hurry to get somewhere else," I said.

"You're getting pretty bad. I'm just a boat, but I'd say you have a mighty big problem."

The wind came up from the coast. I changed course to Monhegan. The wind shifted to the northeast. I changed course for the Isles of Shoals. At three knots it should take us five hours, at two knots it should take us seven hours. At 12:00 noon I was rowing under the umbrella. At one knot it would take us fourteen hours.

"You said you didn't want to go anywhere," the boat said. The heat of the sun was so intense, it kept me under the umbrella. The sea was flat. When the Isles of Shoals appeared, they looked like a prison colony. "There it is," I told the boat.

PRISON COLONY

"That's somewhere, now tell me you want to go there. I see what you mean," the boat replied. The returning wind rippled the water and filled the sails. There were banks of clouds over the land to port and a clear sky seaward. We ran wing and wing between the islands, then jibed into Gosport Harbor. It was crowded. We sailed far into the harbor where the holding ground was said to be good. Two or three boats were rafted together on each mooring. People sat in crowded cockpits and prams. Children were hanging over deck netting dejectedly. Odors of cooking food rose. Music was playing.

"Let's get out of here," the boat said.

"You've caught my mighty big problem," I laughed. We came about and sailed out around the island to find another place to anchor. A research ship was moored off a research station on Appledore. "The hell with research," I told the boat. "They find it, file it, and forget it, unless it can be used by the military."

"Don't anger the Great Spirit with your cynicism," the boat said. We sailed away and left the islands astern, to spend the night at sea. Boon Island was to port. "Nothing there, sail on, sail on," the boat suggested merrily. I lit the lantern and hung it on the boom as the sun disappeared. There were no other lights on the horizon. The sea was as flat as a marble floor and the wind was light. The small mainsail was out to port with the boom lashed to the shroud to prevent it from jibing. The jib was poled out to starboard. The tiller was lashed to a following wind. There was perfect silence. Neither the wind, the sea, the boat, nor I spoke, as though all had been said that needed to be said.

GREAT SPIRIT

"Silence is the voice of the Great Spirit," the boat reminded me. I crawled into my sleeping bag and listened to the Great Spirit until I fell asleep. I awoke when the sun brightened the eastern sky. There was nothing in sight on the horizon. I blew the lantern out and raised the large mainsail. The glare of the rising sun hurt my eyes so I faced aft and sailed by the clouds astern. I didn't know where I had drifted to during the night.

I didn't know where I was. I smoked my pipe and looked for the toothbrush. No luck. I lit a can of sterno and tried to heat some water, stirred in powdered soup, drank it with crackers.

Patches of healthy seaweed drifted by. It was noon. The patches became larger in time, and herring gulls sat in them.

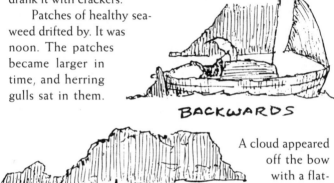

BACKWARDS

SOMEWHERE

A cloud appeared off the bow with a flat-topped island beneath it. "It must be Monhegan," I thought. I checked the chart. I had made good time. The harbor should be to the left. I rounded the headland and sailed to the beach where there was a large sign, "Welcome to Seguin." I pulled out the chart. "Where the hell is Seguin?"

A large sailboat was hanging on the only mooring in the harbor. Sailing close by, I hailed it. "Will the bottom hold an anchor?"

"In by the beach," I was told.

So we sailed for the beach, where two motor launches were anchored. I dropped the anchor close to the beach so the boat could swing in and I could get ashore. I paid out the anchor line. The damn boat started sailing

BOTTOM HOLD ?

and crashed into the two motor launches before I
could get back to the tiller. I gave the boat a piece
of my mind as I dropped the sails.

"You've got a rotten disposition towards boats," the boat replied. "Stop
being so belligerent, damn you!"

I paddled the boat towards
shore as it swung on the anchor, tied
a line to the stern, and leaped out, let-

DAMN BOAT

ting the boat drift away. I secured the other end of the line to
a log on the beach. "Stay there and behave yourself. I want to
find out where we are," I told the boat.

There was a boat shed on the beach with an old railroad
behind it that climbed a steep hill to a lighthouse. I slowly made
my way up to the top where the view was magnificent. Monhegan was on the horizon to the
east. The mainland was to the
west. The south was all

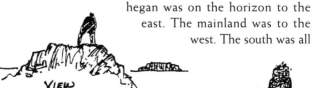

VIEW

ocean. A woman came out of the
house behind me. "Staying the
night?" she asked. "There's a
mooring right down there;
that sailboat will be leaving
soon. Weather will turn

LIGHT KEEPER

bad—three days of rain coming." She wanted to talk.

I didn't want to talk. She could have got a better response
talking to the lighthouse. I made a terse reply and returned to
the boat. Sailboat people are solitary. They avoid people and
sail away from other boats. They usually have very little money

and are referred to as "cheap." Motorboaters are sociable. They motor towards other boats and party. They're big spenders.

By now the sailboat had left. I hauled the anchor aboard and rowed out to the mooring and tied on. For chow I warmed a can of beans with a candle, ate the mess, and sacked out, wrapping in two mainsails and a jib in preparation for the rain. I was tired and slept late.

BEANS

When I awoke I ached all over. Different parts of me were still asleep, and I moved with difficulty. It hadn't rained yet. Apparently the bad weather was still ahead of us. Heavy fog obscured the mainland. I raised the sails, cast off, and sailed by compass toward Fort Popham, a safe haven until the weather cleared. I didn't know the time and couldn't remember the day.

TWO MAINS AND A JIB

"Don't want to know too much," the boat laughed.

We passed buoy #3PI. It was not on my chart. I didn't expect it to be; the chart was ancient. We were being pulled by an unusually fast current with eddies and swirls. I unfolded the chart and found that we were in the mouth of the Kennebec River. The current got stronger, spinning and playing with us until we passed the headland of the fort. Then it flung us aside,

FOG

CIRCLING WATER

PAINTER IN FOG

and we sailed to the dock. "A safe haven from the weather," I told the boat. I looked for the harbormaster, but couldn't find him. They're an elusive breed. Fishermen were casting off the beach. An artist was painting in the fog. Campers were picnicking.

I visited the fort. It was built by Sir John Popham, a gentleman adventurer. He conducted 120 of his kind to this spot in 1606 to establish a fishing colony. Two "shippes," *Gift of God* and *Mary & John*, arrived on August 1. With a favorable wind and tide, the colonists took the "shippes" into the river to find a "fitte" place for their "forte." Their intent was to make their settlement look like a peaceful wooded knoll, but they managed to make it as prominent and hostile as a Norman fortress. It was never attacked in all the time it was

FORT POPHAM

there since it could easily be avoided. The natives were as friendly as the flora and fauna. The bugs didn't even bite. This was truly the "Land of the Saints."

A FITTE PLACE

It was soon discovered that there wasn't a fisherman in the lot. After all, they were gentlemen adventurers, and gentlemen aren't supposed to know one end of a fish from the other. So in December when the liquor ran out and the fun stopped, forty-five of the gentlemen adventurers sailed back to England. During the

FISH?

uncooperative winter, the storehouse caught fire. Naturally, nobody knew how to put it out, so it burned to the ground. That left them in a very bad mood with nothing to do but mistreat the friendly natives. They abused them, beat them, and set their dogs on them. Then they wondered why these pagans became surly and bellicose. The fauna fled. The flowers faded and the bugs began biting. How a benign insect could Darwinly evolve into a savage vampire in such a short time puzzles modern science. Now they are the fiercest in the world and are referred to as "Popham's Curse."

FIRE

BUG BEFORE POPHAM

I put on as much clothing as I could—hat, gloves, and boots—and crawled into the sleeping bag and wrapped myself in the sails, awaiting the attack as the sun descended. They came in a great horde with high

AFTER POPHAM

screeching cries of "Revenge!" "What the hell did Popham ever do to these poor bugs?" I asked myself as I lay there bleeding and scratching. When I decided that there were too many of us aboard, I threw off my wrappings and climbed ashore. "Go bite one another," I told them as I headed for the beach. Fishermen were still standing there with lines in the water. "Fishing that persistently is unnatural," I thought to myself.

BEACH WALKING

I walked briskly all night pursued by bugs. To amuse myself I thought about Columbus and the world before he exposed it for what it was. I think that the shape, size, and land masses of the world were well understood at the time and merely kept secret for trade purposes. Columbus, with his P.R. men and news blitz, let the cat out of the bag in order to do some serious plundering for whoever would back him. I wondered what the country would be like if it had never been "discovered."

By now the sun had risen, and the little vampires returned to their coffins. Spiderwebs appeared everywhere. It was good to see that the bugs didn't have it all their way. "Go get 'em, boys."

WEBS

I was told again that it was going to rain for the next three days. I wasn't going to wait there for it. The tide was low at 7:21. We cast off at 7:30 into a heavy fog. I rowed out into the middle of the river where

RIVER

the swirls spun us like a top while I raised the sails. A large power boat came alongside, and I got that stare that said, "What the hell are you doing out here?" The fog retreated before us as standing waves increased in size. The wind headed us. I tacked and started taking the waves broad-side. I tacked again when the waves became threatening. I thought of sailing inside Ban-tam Rock bell when rocks ap-

STANDING WAVES

peared dead ahead. It was to be expected. If there are rocks around they always get in the way. After several tacks we cleared them and cleared the land as well. We were safe at sea again.

The boat was running before a westerly wind with a beam sea rolling us, when the outhaul fitting let go. I had to lower the main and refas-ten it. Without the sails up the boat would always run

BEAM SEAS

before the wind. If you've tried to raise a mainsail while running, you know the problem. I tied a bucket on a line and threw it off the bow to help point the boat into the wind. It did no good. So I just struggled with it and eventually got it up.

The sun started to bake my clothes. I began to smell like a laundry. Dirt and sweat personalize aroma. A helpful hint to the cruising man: I wear my clothes inside out while sailing, then change them to right-side out when going ashore. That way I keep the good side clean.

DIRT SWEAT SUN LOTION

MESS

Monhegan was off the bow when the outhaul let go again. The wind was strengthening, so I put a reef in the main before I hauled it up. Sorry to say I made a mess of it. We sailed into the harbor right in front of its Grand Hotel. Many people were sitting about on the porch and the lawn. Apparently having seen everything on the island, and with nothing to do but wait for the ferry, they stared at the only moving object in sight. Which was us.

"Let's give them a show of facile seamanship," I said to the boat.

"You do your part and I'll do mine," the boat replied. We

MONHEGAN HOTEL

jibed beautifully before a mooring and stood stationary as I leisurely stepped out on the foredeck, picked up the pennant, and secured it with great aplomb.

A young boy motored by in a pram. "Could you take me ashore?" I asked politely.

"I'm in a hurry," he said, "but if you can come right now I'll take you in." I hadn't done anything to the boat to secure it.

"The hell with it," I decided. "Don't have time." I grabbed the shore bag and stepped out again on the foredeck, but this time my foot caught a line and the boat pitched me overboard. Believe me, that water was cold. I shot out of it like I was on a rubber band.

"You're taking too long," the

PITCHED OVER

boy yelled. "I can't wait." He motored off. There were howls of laughter from the shore.

CAN'T WAIT

"Don't ever leave this boat before you've taken care of it," the boat reprimanded me. I changed my clothes, secured the boat, then hung forlornly out of the cockpit feeding the ducks until a passing lobsterboat took me ashore.

DUCKS

The island was a famous art colony, but paintings could be seen now only in private homes, by appointment. There

was no public gallery and not a single painting to be seen by Rockwell Kent, who gave the island its reputation. A single painter stood on the dock painting the sea. I was disappointed and made for the island's famous forest. With no map and an unerring sense

of direction, it took me no time at all to get lost. Darkness soon came on. I was tired and hungry when I spotted three deer in a clearing and made for them. They bounded off. I followed obediently and soon found myself back at the boat.

LOST

In the beginning of this cruise I had the boat all straightened out and knew where everything was. But early on, we rolled to a good sea and a gust of wind. Everything had crashed around in great fun. Now it was hide-and-seek and peek-a-boo. I made a meal with whatever I could find. Mixed it together, heated it with a candle, then looked for a spoon, fork, or knife. I couldn't find anything. That left me to lap the food out of the pan like a dog.

A light refreshing breeze kept the bugs away. I slept under the open sky and awoke to the sound of a cat mewing. Popping up my head, I said, "Good morning" to the cat.

"Morning," a bearded man rowing by replied.

"Where're you taking the cat?" I asked.

"To Manana Island; he summers there with a fisherman."

"Could you give me a lift ashore when you return?" I asked.

"Gladly." I tidied up the boat and caught my ride.

I ate breakfast at the old Monhegan Hotel amid chatty children, politely smiling elders, and serious adolescents. I enjoyed the meal knowing I would soon enough be back on a diet of beans. From the table I could see the boat. It gave the place character. Perhaps the island should pay someone to sail an ancient boat around the harbor to amuse the tourists. In fact, I could have been paid for yesterday's performance.

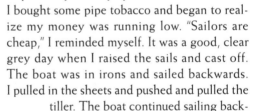
WRONG WAY

I bought some pipe tobacco and began to realize my money was running low. "Sailors are cheap," I reminded myself. It was a good, clear grey day when I raised the sails and cast off. The boat was in irons and sailed backwards. I pulled in the sheets and pushed and pulled the tiller. The boat continued sailing backwards. I sat back helpless, waiting for the boat to decide to do something. The occupant of a passing sailboat yelled, "By God, that's impressive." I waved dejectedly. I should be paid for this demonstration of seamanship.

Only when we cleared the harbor did the boat fall off the wind and sail properly. "Why do you do things like that?" I asked the boat.

"It makes me feel good," the boat laughed.

The wind breezed up. I put a reef in the main. These sails are really too big for the boat. With a reef in, it takes the strain off the shrouds, the boat, and me as well.

The best sailing time is early morning. Evening and night are second best. But avoid that noonday sun. When it came out I took cover under clothes and the umbrella. The boat behaved itself and self-steered nicely. We passed Little Green Island, then Large Green Island. I suspected that there was a larger Green Island ahead. I'm sure the islands appreciate the imaginations of the cartographers.

GREEN ISLAND

Ragged Island was off the bow when there was a loud crash, and the boat groaned. I thought we'd hit something, until I found that the centerboard had dropped. A fitting had let go. I decided to fix it when we got into a harbor. Running before the wind with the centerboard down made steering difficult, but we were close to the island now. There was supposed to be a buoy here, according to the chart, but there was none. The harbor of Ragged Island had fishing shacks on both sides.

RAGGED ISLAND

We came about and tied up to a wharf where I spent some time straightening the boat out. I lowered the jib, leaving it on the forestay, and stuffed it into a bag. Next I lowered the main and lashed it to the boom. Then I raised the centerboard by reeving lines through its pulleys and replaced the broken fitting. I was in no hurry, so I sat awhile in the boat.

When I stepped ashore the wind drifted the boat away from the pilings. I noticed a man standing by a house talking to a woman through an open window. "That's a pretty boat you have there," the woman said. "You brought it in nicely. I watched you, and you took the time to do all the little things you're supposed to do before you left it. That was nice."

I thanked her for the compliment and walked off to explore the island. It was a half-mile long and a quarter-mile wide, but

JEEP

after walking only a short way I stumbled onto a road. A brand new Jeep roared by with a nicely dressed couple aboard. I continued along the road, curious to see where they had come from. At the end of the road stood a vinyl-sided, Tudor-style house with a spacious lawn, plastic chairs on a patio, and a satellite TV dish. Caretaking gulls circled overhead, screaming, "MY property! MY property!"

Turning away from this absurdity, I walked the rugged island shore. The rocks were rounded and weathered. The growth

END OF THE ROAD

was small and desperate. What could survive the winters? It seemed a miracle that life existed here at all. After circumambulating the island, I returned to the boat. The man was still standing by the window talking to the interior.

SAIL TO MATINICUS

CAUGHT

I cast off and sailed for Matinicus. The wind was whipping up white-caps. It was only a short sail, but I managed to catch a lobster buoy on the rudder. I pulled the tiller out and slid the rudder up before the pot tore it off the boat. I should have had a knife handy and cut the damn thing. Two boats from Outward Bound were rafted together in a bay before the harbor. I couldn't sail into them now because of the dead air in the area. Perhaps they'd rather be undisturbed. I would.

I sailed on to the harbor, where the tide was out, leaving only a half a foot of water by the wharf. Pulling up the centerboard, I rowed in and tied up. No one was about. Walking the only road, I passed a sign, "Restaurant Ahead." An old tired truck hob-

EBB

bled by. Two old men waved from it. I waved back. Ahead, on the restaurant door, a sign said, "On Vacation, Back in the Fall." A boy on a three-wheeler sped by, then returned and asked me if I had seen a truck with two old men in it. I pointed in the direction they went. He sped off in pursuit.

The truck re-turned. The two old men waved. I waved in return. The boy on the three-wheeler returned

TIRED TRUCK AND KID

at top speed, pointing questioningly in the direction the truck had taken. I pointed reassuringly at him but doubted that he could ever stop in time to catch the truck.

There were a lot of signs and sounds of building, but I saw no one. I returned to the boat and rowed out to a mooring in the dark. A lobsterboat motored in. I wondered if I was on his mooring. No. He took one beside us. The fisherman grumbled to himself. Swore at the seagull on the stern. Swore at the boat and swore at the ocean.

CUSSIN

"Hello," I interrupted, "will this mooring be used tonight?"

"No, he won't be in. Stay on it." He then carried on his anathematizing. He swore at his catch as he threw it into the pram. Swore at the pram and swore at the oars as he rowed ashore. Before I fell asleep I thought about the wonderfully harmonious communion primitive man has with nature, and that if it wasn't for profanity, he wouldn't be able to talk at all.

I awoke the next day under a clear sky. A gentle breeze filled the sails as I left the harbor out onto an oily, flat sea. A distant fog truncated the islands on the horizon. The wind disappeared. I rowed with one oar tipping the boat to that side. Two islands were off to port. They stayed with us for quite a while, like someone was rowing them too. When I got tired and hot I stopped and had a conversation

ROWING ISLANDS

TRUNCATED ISLAND IN FOG

with two seals who appeared alongside.

"You need all that junk you got on board?" one inquisitive seal asked.

"Only for a short time until I run out, then I'll have to get more junk," I answered. "I'm living on the edge."

The seals laughed and rolled in the water. "Look, he's got clothes, heat, shelter, water,

seals

food, compass, and charts. Nature's ingenuity helps us adapt. He's a misfit, trying to make the environment fit him. We don't need anything. If we tipped that boat over, he'd go to the bottom like a rock."

"I could stay up a while. I can swim."

They flopped around, laughing. "Ingenuity. We don't need to adapt. In fact, most things we know don't have to carry a half-ton of junk around with them to adapt. A big mistake was made somewhere."

"Can you believe this guy? Let's leave him alone—I don't think he's all there."

"He's got to be all there. He couldn't get much more junk aboard that boat."

"C'mon, the weather will take care of him." They swam away laughing and chattering.

"At times like this I wish I was still a tree," the boat said.

We were near the coast again. I couldn't decide where to go. I went forward to put the jib pole up and run for the land. The boat jibed and almost threw me overboard again. "If you want to go somewhere, say so. Don't throw me over the side."

"Pulpit Harbor," the boat said. We headed for North Haven, sailing along its coast looking for the inlet. We found it, farther than I thought it should be. Two schooners were making for the same harbor. I let them pass and then followed.

An osprey nest was on the rock at the entrance. I caught a mooring inside the protected little harbor and busied myself with boat-keeping chores while the wind intensified. I crawled into the sleeping bag and slept awhile. The wind lightened. I decided to sail to Rockport. Tomorrow was the end of my vacation, and it could bring too much wind, or too little. Or the three days of rain could come altogether.

The sun was low when I sailed out of the harbor. It was a short distance, but the wind was against us. We tacked several times through the islands as the wind increased. Darkness came on. The lights on shore gave no sign of distance. I was sailing parallel with the coast when a steady bright white light appeared off the bow. I couldn't identify it. It seemed to be rising higher out of the water as we drew near to it. How close was I to it? I had no idea. I didn't want to tack inshore again where there were no lights and no way of knowing how far off the shore was. I continued on heading for the light, holding up my hand-held running lights.

The red light of Rockport Harbor finally passed abeam of us, and I tacked for it. To this day I still don't know what that white light was. The wind increased as I rounded the lighthouse. Now I was running before a howling wind into an unfamiliar harbor at night. I could only see things that shot past me. I began passing boats. I'd better grab a mooring before I get too far into the harbor. I'm bound to crash into something.

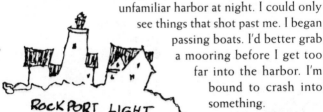

ROCKPORT LIGHT

I hit something. I looked behind. It was a mooring. I jibed and sailed back to it. Missed it to the side. Circled again and rode over it. Tried again, came into the wind, and began drifting backwards as

I ran forward. I hung onto the forestay with one hand and lunged for the pennant buoy. I landed flat on the deck. The bow chock poked me in the chest, knocking the wind out of me, but I hung on.

ROCKPORT

The boat sailed in circles trying to escape. When the line went slack, I cleated it. I cussed the wind, the boat, my seamanship, gasping for air with a painful chest. I rigged my berth and crawled into the sleeping bag fully dressed, grateful to be secured to a mooring.

In the morning I rowed to the dock looking for the harbormaster. There he was, polite and helpful. "Take my mooring over by the Apprenticeshop," he offered. "How long you going to be?"

"A few days, maybe. I've got to go back to Nahant and get a boat trailer," I explained.

"Well, stay as long as you need to." The vacation was over, but Dave Hague had restored my faith in harbormasters.

HARBOR MASTER —

You Ask About The Townie

In your letter of May 4 asking advice about a Townie as a cruising boat, you asked about trailering. I always sail from my mooring at the Nahant Dory Club. I like the feeling of sailing away from home and hate sailing back. So does the boat. When I've sailed as far as I can, I leave the boat and take a bus home. Since I don't have a trailer, I have to beg someone for the use of theirs. Then I drive back and pull the boat out. It takes two people to lower the mast. It's neither hard nor heavy, just clumsy. Then I drive very slowly home, likened to driving

AWAY

LEFT

SLOWLY

your old ailing grandmother over the Rocky Mountains. All her fastenings will loosen up, and secret little things will happen to speed up her demise.

You ask about stability. The Townie is beamy with good stability. I've never capsized it, although others have. I filled it until it was awash, then stood on the gunwale and rocked it. It wouldn't go over, but I have a subtle feeling it will go over on its own when it feels like it, so it can laugh at me when it has

TRYING TO CAPSIZE IT

WHEN IT WANTS TO

me hanging upside down. Townies turn turtle.

You ask about shelter. I throw the mainsail over the boom. Rain pours through it, so I throw an old drop cloth over that. This lets the rain flow on me in a more controlled fashion while the whole thing chatters and flaps in the wind, having given up hope of ever functioning properly and desperately trying to blow away. I've never managed to thwart the elements. I always sit through bad weather and grumble obscenities like a stolid primitive.

STOLID

You ask about cruising arrangements. I've completely lost confidence in my anchor, having dragged it over the bottom of every harbor in the vicinity. I don't rely on seamanship, preparation, or foresight. I squeak through with unmitigated luck, remembering that ancient adage that the gods look down kindly on the imbecile sailor. My advice to you is to take a short cruise to see if you have any luck. If you don't, give up sailing and take up spelunking.

Skill and intelligence help us do the things we want to do, but luck helps us survive to do the silly things again.

You ask about food and water. I've been very reliably told that I can last a lot longer on water than on food. So I bring plenty of water on long trips and never drink any of it. Food is a joke. Peanuts, beans, crackers, and granola. Everything else is emergency rations like the water. I eat everything that disagrees with me. I get stomach pains, gas, nausea, and constipation frequently. I hate eating. A disgusting habit I'd like to get rid of.

FOOD

You ask about rowing—how efficient and how far. Frankly, I row just to give myself something to do, to stop me from going crazy. I row until I'm tired and there's no real progress. If I look at the water, I'm stationary, and it looks as though I'm valiantly trying to push the world by beneath me.

By now you must have concluded that I'm an unsafe, unserious cruiser and that I really haven't any useful information to give you. So, I'll include the boat description you asked for:

ROW OR GO CRAZY

UNSAFE

I didn't choose the Townie. It happened to be for sale for six hundred bucks. The tax refund for that exact amount came in the mail at the time. You could say that the boat and the circumstances chose me. The mainsail is big with a long boom, great for sailing singlehanded in light summer winds. Moderate winds will have you on the rail with a crew. Two is mandatory for racing, or you suffer disqualification. I suffer from disqualification continually. The boat does not like heavy weather and refuses to sail in it.

1   2   3

I put the floorboards across the seats and sleep on the floor. The boat leaks reliably, and I could drown in the bilge water. I've never sailed in other small boats so I'm complacently ignorant of how comfortable I could be.

You ask about my cruising planning. I always sail alone and don't feel overly responsible for the cook, the crew, or the captain (who I don't give a damn for anyway). My date of departure for a cruise is determined solely on impulse.

ALONE

When I feel I must go, I go. The wind decides in which direction I go and the weather decides for how long. I feel safest at an unsafe distance from land. Safe at night with no running lights, just an old oil lantern hanging from the boom.

COOK, CREW, AND CAPTAIN

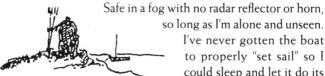

Safe in a fog with no radar reflector or horn, so long as I'm alone and unseen.

I've never gotten the boat to properly "set sail" so I could sleep and let it do its thing. I weigh only 150 pounds, so I reef early so as to avoid the terrifying exhilaration of sailing on the edge. I reduce sail before sunset, regardless of the wind. I don't like playing games with the sail in the dark. I hate engines. They're just noisy little things that help take the boat to the bottom when it takes on water.

THE IMPULSE

REEFED

I can't think of anything else that would help discourage you from taking up sailboat cruising as a recreation. Just watch the weather and learn the names of all the deities. Good luck.

The Appeal

The Townie and I have reached an understanding. After a lot of thinking and long discussions, we agreed that I need a bigger boat. A boat that will take me farther and longer. "After all, it's the next stage of this affliction," I explained to the boat.

I'm tired of standing on the shore staring into the blustery

UNDERSTANDING

winter winds like a half-witted seagull watching the harbor freeze over. Or listening to the weatherman boast, "If you think today's cold, wait for tomorrow, it'll set a record."

"It isn't reasonable to stay in this dismal, gloomy climate," I told the boat. "Animals hibernate. Birds migrate. Flowers and insects sensibly drop dead. This is an uninhabitable place in the winter. Everything has fled or died except me."

The sailing season is over at the end of September, and it doesn't start until the end of June—nine months out of the water. The boats were put in

WINTER

early one year, June 1. That night a storm came up and blew the whole fleet out to sea. Luckily, some were recovered. Otherwise the Town Class would have been lost in Nahant.

The Townie is fine for racing and gunk-holing. But I've had my fill of racing around trian- gles with a leaky boat and ancient sails, searching for a crew every weekend and trying to remember the rules and the things I do wrong so I won't repeat them.

GOING TO SEA

The boat, of course, had a few choice things to say about me. "That's all you want to do is sail with a minimum of repairing, probably because you don't know what end of the nail to hit. You're too cheap to buy a decent set of sails. You've got three sets, and if you put them all up together they wouldn't stop the wind. You're not rational when you sail, but in a continual state of hyper exaltation—wild-eyed and jumping all around. You don't pay attention to essentials and for- get everything you're supposed to remember. The ocean bot- tom is littered with unfortunates who never made mistakes, while you float around like an aborigine doing nothing right. There's a whole maritime heritage that you ignore. How many times have you changed my name? Don't you know it's bad luck to change the name of a boat? Now I'm called *Damn Foole!* You want a bigger boat? Why? To make bigger mistakes. You're a menace to shipping now!"

And I replied, "I've had enough of a cantankerous old Yankee boat. Overcritical, uncomfortable, bossy, falling apart faster than I can fix you up. Considering it a minor miracle if you float when you're launched. And wondering whether I'll make it to shore when white caps appear. Both my arms are longer than they should be from pulling on your mainsheet and fighting your weather helm. You've kept me wet and bailing 'til I've degenerated into an imbecile. But aside from all that, I'll try to give you to someone who will promptly put you in the water **at the** beginning of the season, occasionally sail you out to the islands, and keep you reasonably active in the fleet. Explaining, of course, that you're not a great competitive boat, but a lot of fun if not taken seriously."

Now, to get to this next boat . . . I'd like a kind, knowledgeable boat. A safe, solid boat. A boat that has time on its hands and doesn't care where it goes or how long it takes to get there. A fat, contented boat that doesn't care where it is so long as it's afloat. I've got a feeling that boat has been sitting in a yard neglected, summer after summer. A boat that

FAT CONTENTED
BOAT

88

still has spirit and that only dreads rotting
on its cradle. A character boat, not a
classic. Full keel, 24 or 26 feet long.
Maybe double ended. Maybe gaff
rigged. Cutter or sloop, with a big
cabin and a small cockpit. If I could
find that boat and spend the rest of
the winter messin' about with it 'til
spring, I could outfit it and take

MESSIN ABOUT

some short shakedown cruises through the summer, then head
south in the fall. No plans, just sail. No limit on time or distance. No more winters. I could write stories about it. You
know, I've never anchored in a harbor where I didn't feel like
an intruder. Perhaps a harbor is just
a temporary refuge for a boat,
but we could look for that
elusive harbor we could
feel comfortable in.

I've been searching back-
yards, boatyards, magazines,
and newspapers. It's a good time
to buy, I'm told. Nothing's moving.

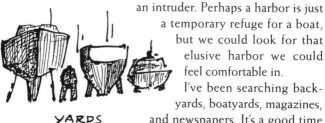

YARDS

Houses, boats, cars. No one's buying. Dollar's dropping. Stock
market's scared. I don't care! It's like telling
me it's a good time to get sicker. I need
that boat. If you have that boat or know
where it is, I'd be appreciative if you'd
let me know where it is. You'll be
in the next story!

SOUTH

A Gathering of the Honorable Mariners

"We sail promptly at noon," I was told. So I arrived at Nahant at 11:00 with my bags. No one was there, so I sat and had time to study the boat. It was said to be one hundred years old—one of those ancient fishing vessels that plied the coast of Maine in bygone days.

At 11:30 the boy arrived. We sat and talked about the coming voyage while the boat radiated its charm and mystery, reminding us of the glorious days when the coastal waters were teeming with life, when nature's forces were used and there seemed to be a kinship between everything. The boy and I traveled comfortably in these memories of the past until the Captain arrived promptly at 12:30, explaining that he had to parade that morning to commemorate one of our ancient and honorable wars.

11:00 AM

BOY AND I

Ancient and

"We're going to have a lot of fun on this trip, lads. Rope work and navigation. Working sails and strange harbors." With a bosun's whistle he piped, "Getting underway." "Cast off the lines." "Boy, here's the log book. That's your job. Write time of departure 1300."

We motored out of the slip to the fuel dock at 1310. We filled the boat's tank and two jerry cans with diesel fuel. "This should last me the whole season," the Captain shouted to all admirers of the past, proud sailboat owners and envious motorboaters. I could see no one but a cynical dock attendant who collected the money and cast us off.

CAST OFF

We motored to a clear area, came up into the wind, took the lashings off the sail, and hauled away at the halyards. The gaff slowly rose, raising the mainsail and drawing it taut. The Captain mumbled continuously with instructions and orders as the two headsails were set. None of the lines could be identified and they criss-crossed one another, making it impossible to tell which was which. "To make it easier to make mistakes, I suppose," the boy giggled.

"That's the way it was, and that's the way it's going to be," the Captain said with finality. The beastly motor was turned off. The boat fell off, and the wind filled the sails. The ancient boat bit into a bow wave and jubilantly charged out of the harbor.

HAUL AWAY

"Get the cannon, boy," the Captain ordered. The signal gun was brought topside, set in place, loaded, and fired with a sharp, deafening roar. The Captain laughed hysterically. "We're away, lads!" And so began this quixotic adventure; an innocent boy, a crazy Captain, and myself on a hundred-year-old windmill.

We beat into a chop towards Winthrop, then tacked and made for Eastern Point off the southern shore of Nahant. From there we could see that the wind was dead on the nose of our course. The boat gave a groan as we turned on the beastly motor in its belly again, heading directly into the wind for Graves Light. The wind lightened but didn't change direction, reminding us that one should never head south in the summer or north in the winter. You'll fight the prevailing winds all the way.

EASTERN POINT

We motored inside of Graves Light, then headed for the solitary spire of Minot's Light, which rises directly out of the sea like the slender neck of a sea serpent. We motored close by on the ocean side. The closer you get, the more impressive it is. Soon after this, we came upon another ancient vessel, under tow. Apparently it was too small to have a belly beast, and the wind was too light for sailing, so it accepted a graciously offered tow from a fishing boat. We followed these two boats into Scituate Harbor.

At its entrance, a gangling figure with a wide-brimmed hat stood atop a flat-topped rock like a sentinel staring at us—welcoming or warning, I know not which. "All harbors should have such figures," I thought to myself, "to greet the weary boatmen."

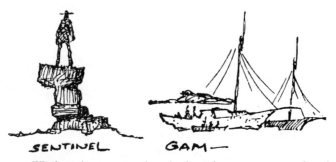

We found a mooring beside the other ancient vessel and were soon gamming with them about the benefits of antiquity, disregarding the fact that neither of us would have made it to port without the assistance of the beast. We secured the boat and rowed ashore. By then the town had closed up. The only things open were three liquor stores and, to counteract the disorder that could cause, the only person on the street was a huge, truculent cop banging his nightstick against everything within his reach. We hurried back to the boat.

TOWN

The boy climbed into his bunk. The Captain smoked cigars and listened to the ballgame on the radio. I stayed on deck to appreciate the night sky. The stars sparkled joyously while the boat swung to the tide in the warm, windless night. When I finally went below, the cabin was filled with smoke. The Captain was asleep with a cigar still in his hand while the radio squawked the jargon of the game. I put the cigar out, shut the babbling radio off, and left the hatch ajar to let the smoke escape.

NIGHT SKY

BELOW

I slept soundly and awoke at 0600. I climbed out a half hour later to find the harbor shrouded in a dense summer fog. We ate a quick breakfast for an early start and cast off, expecting the fog to lift. We motored to the entrance of the harbor, where the fog thickened. The Captain idled the motor.

"What would you do now?" the Captain asked me.

FOG

"Well, since we have a favorable tide and a fair wind, I'd take a compass course to the next buoy, raise the sails, and sail into the fog," I replied enthusiastically. I waited for his agreement.

Instead he looked at me disappointedly as though I had made the worst possible decision, and turned the boat around and motored back to the mooring. When we were safely settled, I took the dinghy and rowed off into the fog.

"Be back when the fog lifts," I was told.

ROWED OFF

I like the seclusion and adventure of the fog, winding my way through the many boats that appear suddenly, to just as suddenly disappear, like shy sea animals. I read the names and the many towns on their transoms, like spices, and failed to remember any of them. I was totally lost and only found my way back when the fog began to burn off.

At 11:30 we motored out of the harbor once again and continued on to Farnham Rock. The boy started playing with the Loran the Captain had recently bought. He was still trying to learn it from the book. I hated the damn thing. It told you where you were every second you were out there. I considered it a spy. In a short time the boy was playing video games on

THE SPY

it, punching in way points, estimating speed and distance. I expected it to start giggling.

"At four knots it should take us seven hours to reach the canal," the boy said.

PLAYING
WITH THE SPY

"Find out the tide, boy," the Captain ordered.

The boy's head disappeared, then reappeared quickly. "It should be favorable when we reach the entrance to the canal," he said.

"Good." We continued on uneventfully, passing well off-shore of Plymouth Harbor. The bells of the Loran rang as we passed way points, sending the boy into fits of giggling. Tow barges and freighters were waiting at the entrance to the canal as we motored through the eddying rip at the breakwater. Then we were caught in the tidal current and swept along.

WAITING

A railroad bridge spans the canal at one point. "Watch that bridge," the Captain told me. "Tell me if it starts coming down."

"Yes, sir." I began staring at it. The current took us rapidly toward it while the bigger ships that had waited were over-taking us.

"Damn!" the Captain shouted. "The bridge is coming down!"

I couldn't believe it. I was staring at it and never was aware it was coming down. Right then I had to admit that there was some-thing terribly wrong with me, and no one else. There were no horns, lights, or bells

BRIDGE

to warn that the bridge was coming down. It didn't matter; I should have seen it.

We slowly came about and hoped the motor could over-come the strength of the current. The boat swerved from side to side as we stayed stationary and the ships backed up behind us.

BRIDGE DOWN

A train passed over the bridge, but the bridge remained down.

"Damn," the Captain said. After a long time another train passed over the bridge from the other direction. Then the bridge rose. All the boats turned, and we continued through.

We left the Cape Cod Canal on the tide and entered Buzzards Bay. I was at the wheel. The Captain was below being instructed by the boy on the uses of the "Spy" Loran. The boat was moving through a series of standing waves caused by the opposition of the wind and tide. The boat began to hobby-horse. Each wave was perfectly positioned to intensify the motion.

BUZZARDS BAY

"Quarter the waves!" the Captain yelled from below as he and the boy were being pitched about. Before I could bring the bow over, it buried itself in the trough of a wave. The quarterboards were torn off as the Captain dashed for the wheel, swearing, "It took me weeks to carve those boards!" By then it was too late; they had disappeared.

I felt responsible and incompetent. "I've got no feel for this wheel,"

QUARTER-
BOARDS

I alibied. "I'm more comfortable with a tiller in a Townie." Small consolation to the Captain. We continued along the thin breakwater to port until it ended. Then we turned into Marion Harbor.

MARION

Disappointingly, there was no statue to greet us at the entrance. Inside, the boats sat in rows like brand new toys. We rowed ashore to a grandiose yacht club. There was no one about. The dock, pool, and tennis courts looked as though

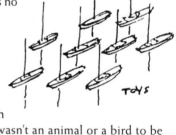

TOYS

they were never used. There wasn't an animal or a bird to be seen. We walked to the center of town where we found a post office, a bookstore, and the Historical Society. Still no one about. In the museum we discovered that the town was connected to the ship *Mary Celeste*. It had artifacts and a description of its mysterious abandonment in mid-ocean. Outside, the only thing that moved was an empty taxi shuttling back and forth on the main street. We returned to the club and rowed back out to the boat. We ate a meal as the sun went down, watching the shore for

MARY-CELESTE

any sign of life. There was none. The town was as much a mystery as the *Mary Celeste.*

The boats swung on their moorings as a light fog settled over them. We turned in, and awoke the next day as the fog lifted. The silence was shattered by the

BACK TO BOAT

roar of the beast as it shook the boat and got us underway. We motored out into Buzzards Bay again. Visibility was perfect, but the Captain, having become familiar with the "Spy," became

SPY

possessed by it. He wanted all the information it could give him—continuously! The boy had to sit in front of it and punch in questions.

"Give me a bearing, boy," the Captain commanded. "What's my distance to the next mark? Am I on course? Give me a time check. What's my dead-reckoning

position?" And so on. It gave me the uncomfortable feeling that I was being watched, followed, and badgered.

Relief came when we anchored in Sakonnet. The boy and the Captain went ashore for a meal to break the monotony of ship's fare. I excused myself by explaining that I had very little appetite and no great appreciation for food. So I went off to walk the beach and explore the abandoned light at the harbor entrance. When I found the path that led to the beach, it was blocked by a large sign. "These Beaches Are To Be Used Only by the Natural Inhabitants of the Township of Little Compton."

SAKONNET

I was puzzled by what a "natural inhabitant" was. The sign continued, "Sand Is To Be Taken Only at Low Tide." This was equally puzzling, since it was not a sandy beach but completely covered with round, sea-tossed rocks. I didn't bother reading on.

An old man sat on a wall nearby. I asked him if he could explain the sign. He replied, "I just arrived here myself. The whole place doesn't make sense to me. Originally, I was taken to Newport and told that's where the money-people lived in the past. Then I was taken here and told this is where the money-people live now."

JUST ARRIVED

SIGN

KEEP OUT   FISHING SHACKS

We sat and looked in wonder at the shingle-roofed fishing shacks overhanging the shore, surrounded by high hedges and manicured lawns. Expensive cars were parked at the ends of long driveways. All the streets were dead-ends with signs prohibiting everything. I walked the beach, then returned to the waterfront, expecting the Captain and the boy to have finished their meal.

I found the boy cringing with embarrassment while the

Captain hopped from table to table, telling Down-East stories. "How much did he have to drink?" I asked the boy.

ENTERTAINING

"Enough," he giggled, pointing to the rum bottle.

Only after the Captain was satisfied that he had properly entertained and questioned all the customers, and complimented all the waitresses, did we get him out of there and into the pram.

"Having fun, lads?" he kept asking us. Before we reached the boat he was bellowing sea-chanties. "Let's fire the cannon," he suggested as we climbed aboard. "Let them know we're here."

SEA CHANTIES

"I think they know we're here," the boy giggled.

"You've got to have fun, lads," he encouraged us as he went below.

"You think he's going to bring up the cannon?" the boy asked, fearfully.

"If he does, let's hope he loads it with a blank charge." The boy's eyes widened. The Captain didn't reappear. When we went below, he was asleep.

"Well, he won't be in any condition to sail tomorrow," I told the boy. We crawled into our bunks confident that we could look forward to a leisurely day.

At sunrise I awoke to the smell of bacon and eggs. "Rise and shine, lads," the Captain shouted cheerfully. "We'll get an early start for Block Island." After breakfast, he fired up the beast and we

RISE AND SHINE

101

motored to the dock to fuel up. "This should do me the rest of the season," he told the dock attendant. We cast off and motored out into another windless day.

I noticed that the compass started spinning crazily. "It'll settle down in a minute," the Captain assured us. "Just the motor affecting it." The boy had just finished writing it up in the log book and put it down to look about.

"That book belongs below, boy! There's a place for everything, and everything in its place!" the Captain chided.

"Where does the book go?" the boy soon asked from below.

"Find a place for it," the Captain said. The boat began rolling as we got farther offshore, and everything below tried desperately to find its proper place. The noise subsided when everything breakable had broken. The Captain puffed on his cigar and grumbled, "Having fun, lads?"

FINDING ITS PROPER PLACE

The wind came up on our nose, so we continued motoring on over the long ocean swells. It was a splendid day except for the noise and vibration from the beast. Soon Block Island appeared on the horizon. We rounded the island to the right and came upon the first channel marker. A two-masted topsail schooner came up on our stern and followed us into the crowded harbor. We motored through the boats

FOLLOWED IN

and found a mooring with a conspicuous "$20" lettered on it.

"Exorbitant!" the Captain screamed. We grabbed it and tied up, while the Captain grumbled about harbor pirates.

We lounged in the cockpit. The Captain smoked his cigar and poured himself a generous rum. I poured myself one too, and lit my pipe. The boy looked longingly at the land. "For

some reason, it reminds me of Fort Sumter," he said innocently, not realizing that he had just started the Civil War again.

LIKE FORT SUMTER

"Lincoln was a great man," the Captain stated flatly. "He made great speeches in cemeteries!"

"Why do we glorify the people who cause the greatest disasters?" I asked.

"He preserved the country," the Captain countered.

"By shattering the laws and shambling everyone's life," I replied, pouring myself another rum.

"Can't have the country split up," the Captain said, filling his glass.

"What was more important, the country or the millions

N. & S.

of people who were slaughtered? The country can be put back together again, but not the people," I said angrily.

"Slaves had to be freed," the Captain said, biting down on his cigar.

"And the only way it could be settled was for everybody to patriotically butcher one another."

"Great men came out of that war."

"They were all pygmies, inept, stupid, and corrupt, still empire-building!"

"Damn you, you can't belittle that great war!"

"That war was disgusting. It was like hordes of insects trying to correct the blunders of the politicians."

The boy looked at us wide eyed, wondering when the fighting would begin. The rum flowed more freely and the argument got more bellicose. We were trapped in the dead past. In a moment of sanity, I declared pompously that if I were on my boat, it would not tolerate this subject.

"What would it do?" the boy asked.

"The Townie would start sinking," I said, smugly. The boy giggled with relief, and the Captain chuckled. The Civil War had ended. We let our minds return to this delightful little harbor as the wind fell away and the sun set. We angelically said good night and tumbled into our bunks while the boat pacified us and rocked us to sleep.

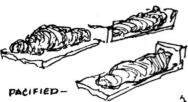

PACIFIED—

0700

We awoke at 0700 to the aroma of hash-and-eggs, coffee, and toast. "We have a little time so we'll go ashore and see the island," the Captain said.

He put the outboard beast on the skiff. "No more rowing," he declared. We motored ashore. The Captain went off looking for charts. The boy and I looked over the boats in the slips along the dock. I looked at the sailboats. They were either too big, too new, too racy, or too luxurious. The boy found what he liked. It was a long sleek speedboat with two of the biggest engines on its transom that I have ever seen.

LITTLE BEAST

BOOGIE IN THAT —

"Now that's what I call a boat," the boy announced admiringly. "I could boogie in that, and nothing would pass me."

"Only something shot out of a cannon," I said. "What about sailing?"

"What about sailing?" the boy giggled.

Later we met up with the Captain. He couldn't find charts. "Whole damn island is changing. Tearing down, building up. Anything stay the same anymore? They sell every piece of junk they can get their hands on. Nothing practical, just junk," he grumbled.

We returned to the boat. "Get out the charts, lads, and give us a course to New London. That's our destination. When we're there you'll see some of the finest sailing craft of the last hundred years."

I responded with an inner cheer. The boy giggled. We raised the sails, cast off, and motored out of the

FOR NEW LONDON

harbor. No one could hear anyone over the noise from the motor.

"Look at me when you speak," the Captain would shout. "I have to see what you say."

There was a fair wind for sailing outside and, thankfully, the devilish beast was shut off. We enjoyed the melodious sounds of the sea, the ship, and the wind. We made for Fishers Island, rounded its eastern point, and entered Fishers Island Sound.

"I've never been in these waters before," the Captain said with worried concern in his voice, "so keep a sharp lookout." The sea was calm, the wind steady, and the visibility excellent. Yet the Captain acted as though these were dangerously uncharted waters. I kept at the chart, plotting our position, and the boy worked the Spy, playing it like Pac-Man. We passed between Groton Point on the mainland and Clay Point on the island as if they were Scylla and Charybdis, the two legendary monsters who sank ships that passed through the straits between Italy and Sicily.

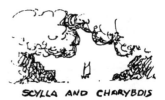

SCYLLA AND CHARYBDIS

The Captain relaxed only when we spotted the lighthouse at the mouth of New London Harbor. It was a quaint little Victorian house rising out of the water, looking as though it had just been carried over from Merry-Old-England, fell off the boat, and was left where it landed. The city of New London was to our port. I expected it to be just like Old London. When we would go ashore, I imagined we would find Charing Cross, Billingsgate, Picadilly Circus, Fleet Street, Cheapside, Rotten Row, and Drury Lane. Another London. We had fled the motherland, only to carry all of its old baggage along with us.

MERRY OLD
ENGLAND

We approached the Yacht Club dock motoring, with the sails drawing in the shifting wind. Orders came voluminously from the Captain. "Tighten up on the outhaul. Luff the jib. Bring in the stays'l a dight.

SMARTLY NOW —

Coming about. Smartly now." I realized this was for the benefit of the spectators.

"She's a hundred years old," the Captain shouted proudly to the crowd on the pier, "and every bit of her is authentic." We did a pirouette before their astonished eyes. Then the Captain shouted, "We're down for the Ancient Mariners' Regatta. Is there a mooring we can take?"

"No," was the curt reply from an attendant.

"There must be a mooring available. We're expected."

"There's nothing. You'll have to anchor," was the answer.

"What kind of courtesy is that?"

"Anchor," the attendant said, and turned away.

We found a place among a nest of power boats and anchored at 1630. The motor was finally shut off and the sails dropped.

IN THE NEST

The boy and I pulled the dinghy up from astern while the Captain pulled the little beast out again and attached it to the stern of the dinghy. We

RELUCTANT BEAST

put the gas can on the dinghy and climbed aboard. The Captain pulled the starter cord. Nothing happened. He pulled again, and again, and again.

"I can row," I suggested.

"No one rows aboard my boat in harbor." Thirty pulls and the motor whimpered. Thirty-seven and it started.

"Cast off." When we did, it stalled. Twenty more pulls and it started. The motor raced, and we charged erratically through the moored boats and up on the beach. In the club-house, the Captain asked the Commodore, "Where do we sign up for the race?"

WHAT RACE?

"What race?" was the reply.

"My God, the Ancient Mariners' Race."

"Know nothing about it."

While the flustered Captain educated the Commodore about the memorable event, I found a shower, and the boy found a phone to call his parents. We met up on the beach, from where swans followed our stammering dinghy back to the boat.

SWANS

The boy rewarded them with biscuits. We had lunch while the Captain entertained us with stories of his nautical adventures in the boat, concluding with, "This boat will be yours one day, boy. It's been good to me; it'll be good to you." The boy looked perplexed.

"What the hell will he do with this boat?" I asked myself, remembering his fascination with the speedboat. The sun set, and I took the dinghy for a row.

"Have fun, lad," the Captain said.

The silence and the solitude of the small boat was comforting. When I returned to the boat later there were four Captains in the cockpit, all smoking cigars and as drunk as they could get in that short time. They were admiringly extolling one another's achievements and abilities.

"I got to admire you for building your own boat," one Captain would say.

"Well, I had tools," another replied.

"You built yours without tools," a third offered.

"I had help and a place to build—you didn't."

"Sometimes that's harder than building one."

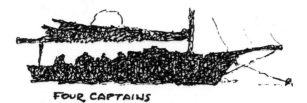

FOUR CAPTAINS

It went on. I went below. The boy was asleep. I lay in my bunk and heard the bull session break up. Soon the Captain stumbled down the hatch mumbling, "Gonna rain." He slammed the hatch tight, then lay in his bunk and smoked his cigar, filling the cabin with smoke, chuckling over the stories he hadn't told yet. Too tired to care, I fell asleep.

CIGAR

"0800, out of the sack, lads," the Captain roused us out. "Jesus jumped-up Christ, let's get this mess cleaned up." Topside there were rum bottles and coke cans, plastic cups and beer cans, cigar stubs and matches. The cleanup and the breakfast, with more of the Captain's nautical narratives, brought us dangerously close to the time of the start of the race.

We started the motor-beast, cast off, then set sail when clear of the mooring area. We motor-sailed down the main channel to the city pier, where we anchored again.

"I'm going ashore," the Captain announced.

"Should we come too?" I asked.

"No, this is a skippers' meeting."

So the boy and I stayed aboard and watched the other ancient boats assemble around us. It was a strange assemblage indeed. A launch picked up the Captain, took him ashore, and brought him back a little later. He handed me the instructions.

SKIPPERS MEETING

"Read these; they're your responsibility."

I thought to myself that it would have been much easier if I had gone

OTHERS

ashore and heard what was said. He was probably too busy telling stories to have heard anything. I began reading.

"Set the topsail," the Captain ordered. "Hop to it; we haven't got much time. Haul up the main and jib. Cast off. Coming about. Let go the jibsheet. What do the instructions say about the start?"

"I haven't read them yet, haven't had time."

"Damn it. I can't do everything," the Captain complained. "A flag is up on the committee boat—what is it?"

"Blue."

DAMN IT.

"That means ten minutes to start."

"The instructions say five," I replied.

"Ten minutes," he insisted. "Plot the course and give me range and bearing. We've got to work together, lads. Coil that line. Harden up on the main. Coming about. Let the jibsheet go. Not that one, boy, that's the stays'l."

"I can't tell the difference," the boy replied.

"The red flag is up—that's the start!" I yelled.

"It can't be," the Captain said.

The starting gun was heard. All the boats headed for the line. We were running the line on a close reach. We had good speed and only had to head up to cross the line with a perfect start.

RED FLAG

"Great start," I shout. We were in the lead, but the boat began to fall off. I looked around and found that the Captain was not at the wheel. I rushed back and grabed the wheel.

STEERS HERSELF

"Let it go," he said, "this boat steers itself."

"But other boats are getting to windward of us."

"That doesn't mean anything; we're faster."

The wind lightened as we made for the harbor entrance buoy. "I've got them all covered," the Captain laughed maniacally. A larger boat pulled alongside to windward.

"We've got him in the hopeless position: he can't pass us; we're backwinding his mainsail. Just stay on course," I said, getting carried away.

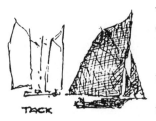

TACK

"Who's captain of this boat? You want to take the wheel?" the Captain asked.

"Just offering advice," I said.

"Luff the sails and prepare to tack."

"What? You'll let them take the lead!"

We luffed up and tacked over, letting the whole fleet go by. I couldn't believe it. I was about to scream angrily, "You just let the whole fleet escape; we're not in this race anymore, we're on a flyer." But I remembered in time that the hardest thing to do in this world is to keep your mouth shut.

"Where am I? Find my latitude and longitude," the Captain commanded me.

I couldn't contain my anger. "I'm not playing with that God-damned voodoo box!"

"I have to know where I am," the Captain said desperately.

"You're right by the entrance buoy," I said through clenched teeth, pointing to the offending object.

POSITION

"Not satisfied," the Captain stated authoritatively, "I want to know exactly where I am."

"Bullshit," I growled. The boy played with the Spy and found the lat and long. The flooding tide was now stronger than the wind.

"We are approximately one mile from the first mark," the boy reported. "Doing .06 knots, and in the last thirty minutes we made a good %₀₀ of one mile." A distant foghorn heckled us.

"Plot the T.D., lad, I've got the lead boat scared. He's pinching like hell. Work with me lads, I'm trying to keep this boat moving."

We were as stationary as the channel buoy beside us. The radio announced that the race was canceled.

"What?" the Captain shouted. "I've got this race won. Get our lat and long,

STATIONARY

boy, and I'll radio the other boats and tell them to take theirs. We'll see who's won this race!"

"You can't win a race without rounding all the marks properly and going over the finish line," I declared.

"The racing doesn't matter, lad, just that we're having fun. That's all that matters. Got the lat and long and time, boy?"

"Yes."

"Good. I'll radio the other boats. Even if somebody's ahead of us they have to work in our handicap."

"How is that determined?" I asked.

"By a little cheating."

"I've concluded that all racing is an involved process of cheating and that there is very little sportsmanship in sports."

"The racing doesn't matter," the Captain declared again.

"No, the cheating does."

"You've got to enjoy it, lad," the Captain laughed.

The boat roared and we motored back to the anchorage. In the process of lowering the sails, the tops'l was fouled and the gaff jammed. These problems were eventually solved with much swearing and pulling. Then the halyard broke, and the whole mess fell down.

A launch sped out from the clubhouse and came alongside. The boy disappeared below, reappearing with his bags. He leaped aboard the launch and embraced his parents.

"Come aboard," the Captain invited.

"No time," the parents shouted as the launch raced off with the grinning kid.

"That's what that desperate phone call was all about," I thought to myself.

BOY LEAVING

"I need a drink," I said.

"Good idea," the Captain agreed.

In no time at all we were embroiled in a drunken argument. "How can this boat be an authentic antique," I asked, "when it has a diesel engine, dacron sails, roller reef jib, loran, and an aluminum mast? Not to mention that you probably replaced every piece of wood on it."

"You know the old story about the axe," the Captain laughed. "Fellow had an axe. Claimed it was a hundred years old. The handle had been replaced six times and the head three times. But it was still the original axe, a hundred years old. Let's go ashore for the awards."

AUTHENTIC

We climbed into the skiff and cast off. Forty pulls on the starter cord. The little beast didn't give off a sound. The Captain sat back, winded.

"Want a tow?" a passing ancient mariner offered.

"No one tows me," the Captain shouted truculently, and starts pulling on the cord again.

I tossed the towline to the passing boat. The Captain pulled the starter cord desperately all the time we were being towed. The motor kicked over. They threw off the towline as we raced by them. Soon the little beast coughed and died. The line was handed back to the tow boat while the rabid Captain continued to pull on the cord. Just before we reached the dock, the beast kicked over.

TOWED

"Throw off the towline," the Captain ordered. The two boats bump the dock. The Captain grumbled with satisfaction. "Tie up. I'm going to see what's been decided about the race." He charged up the gangway, and in a short time I could hear an argument over the results of the canceled race.

The ancients assembled in the club room. The most ancient of the ancients silenced the argument. "Brethren, I've got these awards, and I'm damned if I'm going to take them home with me again this year. So in order to shut up the loudest skipper in the fleet, we're going to give him first place!"

Loud applause. The Captain proudly stepped forward. "And don't make a speech," the ancient warned.

AWARD -

"Thank you, but this'll never shut me up. There should be no doubt I won that race. Besides, it's all in fun. It's the comradeship that matters . . ."

"Oh, for God's sake, shut up and let me get rid of the rest of these," the ancient said with good-natured irritation.

From this experience I have resolved to always sail alone. One miserable son-of-a-Sinbad on a boat is enough. And this miserable son will never think of racing ever again.

EVER AGAIN

Tom's Coast of New England

BEING AN ACCOUNT
OF A CRUISE ALONG
THE NEW ENGLAND COAST
ABOARD THE VESSEL
THE *DAMN FOOLE II*

The Author admits to free and blatant pilferage from "Carter's Coast of New England."

On one of the coldest, drizzliest, dreariest evenings in mid-July, I paid a visit to my friend, the Professor, at his residence on the seacoast of Nahant. The study of sailing had been his passion from early boyhood. His house abounded in objects of the sea. The rooms were cluttered with nautical paraphernalia. There were pictures of ships and harbors and ancient charts

adorning the walls. Sails were being made, repaired, or altered, boats planned for construction. A prodigious library of the history of sailing provided him with a knowledge of every sailing craft that put to sea.

The Professor greeted me amiably, although he commented on my bilious appearance.

THE COAST

"I can stand this weather no longer," I declared biliously. "It has put a fever in my veins that made me terminate my employment; and until a social system is devised that a person of good conscience can participate in without shame or regret, I shall not work ever again. Meanwhile, I intend to start on a cruise along the coast of Maine next week. You had better come along if you do not wish to languish here. I can assure you it will be the finest cruising you have ever done. The scenery will be superb. Huge rocky cliffs rise right out of the water. It is the wildest coast imaginable. The haunt of every kind of sea bird—"

"Will there be whales?" he asked.

"I promise you we shall see whales in abundance. They are feeding on Stellwagen Bank as we speak and will be there until October when they migrate to southern waters. You shall see harbor seals and porpoises and at least one specimen of every creature that inhabits the great deep. I have written to my friend in Swampscott who knows of a good boat that is for sale. It is a sloop; stout, tight, and roomy with four berths. She measures 19 feet overall and draws 2 feet, 7 inches. It had been sailed much before being damaged in

THE VESSEL

a storm. The mast is broken, but the hull is sound and had not been holed. She is in a boatyard at Winthrop. I shall tow her here to Nahant, have the mast repaired and the vessel outfitted. You had better get ready at once for I shall be off in a flash the moment arrangements are made."

"How long should we plan to be gone?" he asked.

"It will be of at least a month's duration," I replied.

The questioning continued until midnight, when I left him in an agitated state of indecision.

Next day I found the boat in an old boatyard far from the water in Winthrop. The tide had turned at the top of the flood when the truck arrived to take us to the water. A wheel fell off the truck before it could be done. I wondered if this was the beginning of bad luck that would pursue the boat. But just before we lost the water, the truck was repaired and the boat put in.

A Pilot and an Experienced Waterman towed us under bridges, out the channel, around Deer Island, and across Broad Sound to Nahant Bay. Secured to a mooring, we took the mast off to be repaired. I asked the Pilot and the Waterman to sign aboard for the cruise. They bluntly refused, wishing me well and offering spiritual guidance.

"I'll gratefully accept your spiritual companionship, leaving your guidance ashore," I retorted.

Two days later, the Professor came to see me and somberly declared that he must decline my invitation. He dourly admitted that he had too many trifling commitments and that he was resigned to languish in petty creature comforts by the cemetery gate awaiting to be called by our divine lord high executioner.

"I can go only in spirit," he added pathetically.

The Piscatologist from Swampscott, who had helped me purchase the boat, soon arrived. He too apologized for not being able to accept my offer.

"Then I'll regret the absence of you both but welcome two more spirits aboard," I said resolutely.

It rained the night of July 18, leaving a fog fighting with the sun for dominion over the next morning. As soon as the sails were raised, the lines were cast off from shore by my corporeal crew. Immediately, the spirit crew and I were going with wind and tide across Boston Harbor, accompanied by sailing ships of all classes and dimensions. The Parade of Sail was commemorating the anniversary of the discovery of America in 1492. Barks and Brigs and fully rigged ships. Schooners and Caravels. Roman Galleys and Viking Longboats, Irish Hookers and Chinese Junks. Dromens and Carracks. Hoogars and Botters, Ulaks and Umiaks, Jangadas, Mulettas, Brawleys, Scaffies, Gyassas, Gozoes, and Xebecs. Every nation in the world was celebrating the exploitation of a continent.

WITH WIND & TIDE

PARADE

By noon the light westerly wind had lightened, the sea flattened, and the sails flapped as we ghosted toward Scituate. All the while the spirit crew had baited hooks dangling in the water, sitting transcendentalized, until the Professor pulled aboard a

SPIRITS FISHIN

dreadful conglomeration of growth and garbage. The Piscatologist subjected us to a detailed description of every article with its impressive Latin title, exasperating me to the point where I pitched the mess back into the sea and put the oars in their locks.

I began rowing, ordering the others to do likewise. The sun grew hot at noon, and they soon complained vociferously of thirst, reminding me that one the things I had forgotten to bring was water. In time, clouds mercifully covered the sun, letting us sink for solace within ourselves as we rowed on.

BACK INTO THE SEA

The wind reappeared from the south at 4:00, increasing to a good southwesterly breeze by 6:00. This is the best time of day for sailing. I enjoy the evenings and early mornings. When we rounded the light at Scituate Harbor, a catboat followed us in like a companionable pet. At

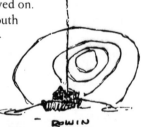
ROWIN

the public dock, we were instructed to take a mooring across the channel, away from the carnival that was on the landing.

CARNIVAL

"You came at the right time," we were told. "There will be fireworks at midnight."

The mooring was familiar to me. I had hung on it many other times. The name on it was *Farnsworth*. It had an ancient chain, ball, and pennant covered with growth

120

MOORING

from which the Piscatologist collected samples. The Pilot slowly filled and lit his short black pipe, stuck it securely in his mouth, and cooked soup. We ate, listening to the screams and laughter of the carnivalarians, and later watched the fireworks.

By then we were all very tired but nevertheless found enough energy to belligerently argue over sleeping arrangements. I obtained the starboard quarter berth with no certainty of permanence. We slept soundly until 6:00 Sunday morning. Readying the boat, we sailed to the dock and gave the public motor launch a good palpable hit.

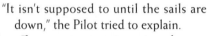

GOOD HIT

"This damn boat never stops when it's supposed to," I complained.

"It isn't supposed to until the sails are down," the Pilot tried to explain.

"I mean at a mooring, at anchor, or tied to a dock. It just keeps sailing."

The crew ignored me and went ashore to breakfast on toast and coffee.

Thunderstorms were predicted for the afternoon. Undaunted, we returned to the boat and raised the sails, cast off, and sailed out of the harbor. The wind was light and behind us, which left us in the heat and the haze rolling in the wake of noisy powerboats. It was still a good sail to Plymouth, with the tide adding a knot to our speed. Discovering that we had no details of the harbor when we arrived, we followed other boats in. At

CLOUDS

the inner harbor we could not stem the ebbing tide and, until it lessened, we let the boat drift. Soon the wind strengthened, letting us tack up the narrow channel.

We hit bottom twice but managed to free ourselves. The wind was blowing hard now, and we wished we had the small jib up instead of the genoa, which continually caught in the shrouds and took too long to be pulled around when coming about, trying to avoid the incoming fishing boats. We passed the last buoy and inquired about a mooring. "Twenty-five dol-

DORY

lars," we were told.

We anchored and, with no way to get ashore, we stayed aboard. Late that evening a dory brought out the Artist accompanied by the Assyrian, as his friends are wont to call him. We sat on deck for hours with a spectacular view of the *Mayflower II*, a facsimile of the vessel that brought the Pilgrims here.

Naturally, the conversation turned to that event. "There was not a farmer or a fisherman or a hunter among them. How did they expect to survive?" the Assyrian stated.

MAYFLOWER

"They were supposed to have landed here in the spring and not the winter. They were inexcusably delayed by the adventurers haggling over their intended profits," the Professor added.

"They were shanghaied," the Pilot insisted. "They were supposed to land in Jamestown, where preparations were made to accept them, but the Captain was told to dump them in New England so the adventurers could establish a new charter, thereby increasing their profits."

"They came here to practice their own religious and social intolerance," I said.

"Everything was done wrong that could have been done wrong," the Professor said cynically.

"They should have tore off their clothes and waded ashore naked. Left everything of Europe on the ship and burnt it," the Artist added imaginatively. "They would have been accepted by Native Americans and taught their ways. To fish, hunt, and farm. The country was truly free then, and offered a new life. The Statue of Liberty would have been an Indian, hand raised in welcome, not a Greek goddess with book and torch. All would be greeted by the short, sincere welcome of an aborigine rather than the hollow political rhetoric of today that is as artificial as the image."

Our conversation did not cease until moonrise, when the Artist and the Assyrian declined to sail with us, agreeing to join the spirit crew. They went ashore leaving me to argue with all the spirits again over berthing arrangements. The port after-quarters were filled with the Piscatologist's specimens. I tossed them out and enjoyed a good night's sleep.

WELCOME

In the morning we were aground at anchor, surrounded by shallow-draft catboats. We freed ourselves, though the tide was on the ebb, and sailed out into a thick fog without a chart. We tried to follow other boats, all of which quickly disappeared. We rounded a buoy that I suspected was the last, leading into the outer harbor. It wasn't the last buoy, as it turned

AGROUND AT ANCHOR

out, and we ran hard aground. All aboard jumped over the side to help get free. We pushed, pulled, rolled, and rocked the boat, but the tide this time dropped too quickly and left us securely in the mud.

"Good fishin' there," we were told by a passing boat. This suggestion immediately had the spirit crew engrossed in that genetically addictive pastime, fishing

~ AGROUND ~

even though there ain't no fish. I walked out and planted an anchor and then busied myself aboard, stowing things away.

"Everything aboard a vessel has its proper place," I was told by the Pilot, "which ain't the same on all vessels, and it's a minor miracle when the proper place is discovered."

In the process I happened to turn the chart over and found a detailed enlargement of Plymouth Harbor. "We're aground on Splitting Knife Shoal," I told the Professor, showing him the chart. This information provided him with the opportunity to explain everything we did wrong.

"I don't want to hear any more," I told him, hoping to cut his pedantic prattle short.

"We should examine our mistakes unabashedly and learn from them; otherwise, they're worthless," he continued.

"We have millions of years of mistakes behind us, and the only thing we've learned from them is that we haven't learned a damn thing of any importance."

$10.00
TIMEPIECE

I wound the ten-dollar alarm clock and shook it to remind it. The incoming tide and the wakes of passing boats freed us by 11:00.

The flag atop the lighthouse on the headland was straight out. We raised all sails only to find that the wind was not quite strong enough to stem the now flooding tide. We gave up trying to escape that accursed harbor. We headed for Saquish Head, running aground twice more, setting out anchors, and kedging off. Stormy cumulus clouds hid the sunset when we finally anchored.

TRYING TO ESCAPE

"No shore leave again," the Pilot announced. The Assyrian bemoaned another night of abstention. We supped heartily on beans and crackers. The wind soon increased, and the Pilot advised me to drop a second anchor, which I did. In the candlelit cabin I confessed to being very tired. I received no sympathy, and wondered openly why we were all out here.

"There's no place else to be," the spirits chanted in unison. "And nothing else to do."

The halyards started making an awful clatter, demanding that I go topside again and tie them away from the

WHY ARE WE HERE?

mast. It was a cold, clear night with a cutting wind, and it was good to get below. I never had a below in my previous boat, a Town class.

Still, I had to tumble out of my berth many times to tie

down all the things that go bang in the
night aboard a boat. I was awake at sunrise but didn't want to get up.

"Take warning, shipmate," the Pilot
cautioned me. "The third day aboard

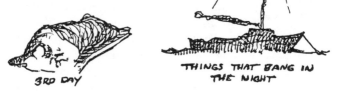

3RD DAY

THINGS THAT BANG IN
THE NIGHT

a boat is a hurdle. You find that you want to go home to a familiar place; see, hear, touch, and smell familiar things. But get
by that third day and everything aboard becomes familiar. The
boat is now home."

We hauled anchor. The wind was light and the sea flat as
it should be. Sanctimonious cormorants
crowded on a rock watching us intently
as we escaped the harbor. "Puritan sal-
vagers ready to pick the carcass of our
boat when we abandon hope,"
the Pilot commented.

We made course for
the Cape Cod Canal.
But the uncooperative
wind shifted into the south,

CORMORANTS

making our southerly course impossible. The crew called for a
vote, the result of which was that we set sail for Provincetown,
twenty-five miles away.

Ominous clouds piled up in the west, rumbling with thunder. We took all the sails down in preparation and sat in the
cockpit. The storm overtook us at 2:30, raining heavily, with no
wind. It rained harder, pounding the sea flat. Thunder grumbled

1ST STORM

as lightning flashed all about us. In a half hour the storm had ended, leaving us cold and wet and frightened.

I glanced to the west again, and it was black as night, grumbling insanely. A huge bolt of lightning came straight down out of the sky into the water a mile astern of us. That did it. The crew and I clambered below, closed the hatches and lit the candles, each of us comforting himself the best he could.

I thought of the many pleasant sunny sailing days I'd had. The Artist dreamed of a permissive patron. The Assyrian remembered days when he was happily drunk. The Piscatologist's thoughts went back to when there still were fish in the ocean. The Pilot thought of how he could embellish this storm into the greatest lie

THROUGH THE HATCH

he had ever told. The Waterman prayed to every god he could think of to preserve his miserable life. The Professor talked about the atmospheric phenomenon of a storm as though knowledge was his safeguard. The clock stopped and had to be shaken vigorously. We waited for the worst.

The second storm's heavy rains pounded on the cabin top, trying to get at us. The lightning flashed simultaneously with the rumbling of thunder. The storm was short but extremely violent. We were still afloat when it ended. Anxiously looking to the west again, we saw it was clear and sunny, but to the north and south of us storms swept by all day. By 6:00 we should have seen land, but we saw none. It was getting late. By 7:30 we heard a foghorn and saw the top of the Pilgrim tower above the haze.

We sailed against the tide in light air. The sun set and the wind disappeared. We bent to the oars silently as the night came on. I flashed on the running lights only when other vessels approached.

2ND STORM

At 10:30 we rounded the breakwater and anchored. We ate soup and slept where we were when we finished.

When I went on deck the next morning, the village of Provincetown stretched before us. I immediately roused the crew and prepared to sail into shallow water, wade ashore, and examine the peculiar inhabitants. "It's the migratory flyway of tourists," I explained to my passengers. They remained unimpressed.

PROVINCETOWN

BOY IN A BOAT

A boy in a boat came by and offered us a lift in. We tied the sails back up and climbed aboard. The boy said he lived on a 32-foot Bristol he had bought cheaply but wished he had a smaller boat like ours. "I think I would sail more," he confessed.

"Small boats do sail more," I agreed.

He had two prams on shore and offered the use of one. He would leave the oars.

Ashore, the Professor went to the library; the Artist visited the galleries; the Piscatologist went to the fish pier; the Pilot, Waterman, and Assyrian went to a tavern. I rented a bicycle and rode quickly away from the lot of them.

The bike path took me to the museum in the dunes. At the observatory it was explained that after we cut down all the trees, the soil washed away and these desert dunes advanced as over the ravaged land of Neneveh. We are now patiently watching and waiting for the corpse to revive, while we fish out the ocean and pollute the air, no doubt to watch them try to revive at some future date. We stand monitoring and overanalyzing, collecting volumes of data and do next to nothing. Education has become a goal unto itself to do nothing with. I should have gone to the tavern and gotten drunk with the Assyrian and his companions.

We all met at the beach quite late, the Pilot, Waterman, and Assyrian properly drunk. I complained of their excessiveness while taking what I thought to be "the other pram." We rowed out to the boat and tied the pram to the transom. I prudishly complained again of the drunken conviviality of the spirits. My dour mood left me with the feeling that something was wrong, and we could only wait to discover it.

At 6:00 the next morning a boat crashed into us. "Who gave you permission to use that pram?" an angry fisherman shouted. "I missed two hours of work looking for it. Look at this boat. It's a mess. What kind of a sailor are you? I don't care how far you came. Get this piece of crap out of the harbor." He untied his pram and motored away, not waiting for an explanation.

"There really was none if it truly was his pram," the Pilot accused me.

ANGRY FISHERMAN

Later we sailed to shallow water, put our clothes in a bucket, and waded ashore. We separated again, each pursuing

STEALING CORN

his own interest. I walked to Indian Hill. The *Mayflower* made first landfall at the Cape and anchored in Provincetown, where, it was recorded, the first act the Pilgrims committed upon coming ashore was to steal the Indians' winter cache of corn, leaving nothing and never thinking it improper to let "savages" starve.

Later I met the angry fisherman on the beach. He was still angry. I apologized and explained the mixup. He preferred to remain angry. So I gave him reason to remain angry.

RATHER BE ANGRY

"You are in the wrong business, my friend," I told him. "Fishermen and farmers, although necessary for our survival, are doomed to poverty. The harder they work, the poorer they get. The catch each year gets smaller because of pollution and overfishing. And crops get smaller because the soil becomes depleted and less fertile."

"I am a fisherman," he responded proudly.

130

"You're a fool," I told him. "Money is made by manipulation, not work."

I offered him money for the misuse of his pram. He adamantly refused, stomping off a happily angry man. I spoke with his wife, listening to her litany of poverty. I gave her ten dollars.

"He'll be more angry if he learns I took the money."

"I can't imagine him being any happier."

I was determined to leave the next day. The Assyrian came aboard, drunk again. I complained. The next morning I read in the ship's log, "The Captain is sober again this morning." From then on it would be the first statement in the log each day and, since entries in the log may not be changed, the insinuation would remain. The Pilot went ashore to fill our water firkins, find more charts, and get weather information. The Artist fraternized with members of his peculiar species. The Professor lost himself in the library. The Assyrian and Waterman got drunk.

LOG

All returned to the boat reluctantly. We hoisted the anchor at noon—a late start. The Piscatologist dredged for marine grown on the bottom as we left the harbor. He was rewarded with trash, garbage, and broken gear, and finally lost his dredge on a wreck. The harbor was a dumping ground.

DREDGE

We made course for the Cape Cod Canal again. It was a long, uneventful sail with the land astern never seeming to leave us, nor the land ahead drawing near. When the sun set we were still far offshore.

The night was black as night could be. In the darkness the land came upon us quickly, and because there was no surf on the beach we could not tell how far off this unfamiliar shore we were. As a precaution, we dropped the anchor twelve to fifteen feet, letting it hang, and continued toward shore until it caught and set. Then we paid out scope and dropped another anchor. The sails were lowered. The Pilot cooked something, and we ate whatever it was and lay in our bunks by 11:30.

"You told me that we were to cruise the coast of Maine. Why in heaven's name are we trying to go through the Cape Cod Canal?" the Professor asked.

"I thought we would sail Buzzards Bay, visit Cuttyhunk in the Elizabeth Islands, then Martha's Vineyard, Nantucket, Chatham, then through Monomoy Gut out into the Atlantic and up the outside of the Cape back to Provincetown, then across Stellwagen Bank to Gloucester. From there we would start up the coast to Maine," I explained windily.

TO MAINE!

"An ambitious prelude to the coast of Maine," he chided.

"How do you expect to get through the canal?" the Pilot asked.

"In the morning we'll sit at the entrance and ask passing boats if they'll tow us through."

The spirit crew looked at me quizzically, then retired.

I was up at sunrise and underway. The spirits slept late. We sailed to the canal entrance and waited. In time, several boats passed and refused to tow us. I offered money and was still refused by other boats. A Coast Guard boat came out in a flurry.

No!

Manned by two young men and a woman in uniforms, they came alongside and stared at us, not saying a word. By doing so they were demanding an explanation.

"I'm waiting for a tow through the canal," I offered as justification for my presence there.

"Do you own that boat? Where are you from? When did you get here? Do you have a radio?" they asked.

Ignoring the questions, I asked if they could tow us through.

"We don't tow," was their helpful reply.

By now I was getting angry and was cautioned by the Pilot to be courteous. "They obviously want to arrest someone rather than help and would do so for the slightest and most obscure transgressions."

In 1872 the Life Saving Service was formed by the Humane Society—private citizens who volunteered time and contributed money. In 1915 it was taken over by the government and turned into this police force peopled by robots who are given no authority to make a decision. Functioning like protective nannies to every passing boat. Arresting anyone for violations of safety and negligence. "Is there a towing service?" I asked tersely.

"No," they answered.

In days past all vessels were towed through the canal. Now that is completely discontinued and everyone is left to his own devices. You must own everything you use in this world; that is why we are buried in junk. Prisoners of our precious privacy.

The patrol boat circled us several times, then raced away to make its official report. By now we had lost the tide that would have quickened our transit of the canal. At noon we abandoned

IN DAYS PAST

hope and set sail for Barnstable Harbor. The Pilot suggested that the harbor was too long and narrow and the wind not favorable. I studied the chart and concurred. We sailed past and approached Sesuit, a small harbor a short distance down the coast. We beat into the narrow channel and, fearing to go farther in where it narrowed even more, we docked at a nearby boat club. I inquired about anchoring for the night and was told by a very helpful commodore to stay on the dock for the night. There was ample water to keep us afloat and if there was anything further he could do for us we should let him know.

Everyone had left by sunset so we settled down for a quiet evening, eventually retiring. In the small hours of the morning there was a grinding sound. I ignored it. When it grew louder and persistent I went topside to find the boat stuck in the mud, the dock lines holding us upright. I eased up on them, afraid they would snap or pull out fittings, but the boat started to fall over. I quickly retied them, then got every line I could find and trussed the boat up like a criminal. The bow sank deeper into the bottom, pointing the stern into the air. A sliver of moon smiled at us, amused. With nothing else to do I went below and tried to sleep in the bunk that put me in a standing position. The grinding stopped and the straining lines held the boat in traction.

At sunrise a rabbit on the dock greeted us, viewing the amazing sight with his starboard eye. After a time we were afloat but landlocked. In another hour I was able to pull the boat into deeper water and raise the sails, and we drifted out of the harbor on the tide.

AMAZING SIGHT

The wind was light from the west. An iodine

haze hung over the power plant by the canal. The tribal bonfire kept burning in the cave. The Professor brought our attention

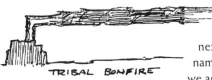

TRIBAL BONFIRE

to a blackheaded laughing gull sitting in the water next to us. "A ridiculous name for a beautiful bird," we agreed.

We sailed the twenty miles to Provincetown, where we spent the night. The next day we sailed over Stellwagen Bank in the hope of seeing whales. We saw many whale watch boats crowded with cetacean voyeurs.

We made a good passage with a stiff breeze to Salem. We docked at Derby Wharf and went ashore to the witches' monument designed to commemorate

NO WHALES

the three-hundredth anniversary of the witch trials. It was constructed not at Gallows Hill, or at the court house, or where the accused were imprisoned, or even in Salem Village, which is now Danvers. The monument is in the graveyard where the Judge is buried.

The Professor told us of the last witch tried in Salem Village. The woman was taken off the street and put in the dock. She was repeatedly accused of witchcraft, which she repeatedly denied until, exasperated, she shouted, "You would have me be a witch?"

"Aye," was the reply from the court.

"Then how do I be a witch?"

"Why, it is common knowledge. Repeat, 'I am a witch' three times."

The accused woman repeated it loudly three times. "Now

I am a witch. You can only try to punish the innocent. You will not try a real witch."

"You dare to threaten this court? Make no mistake, you may only do what you are permitted to do in this court."

"So you say, but I'll do as I wish," she replied angrily. "Question me," she demanded.

"Are you an evil witch?"

"Aye. I am that now. A bitchly evil witch."

"Did you blast our crops and make the soil infertile?"

"I did not, but I do now."

"Did you make our cattle give sour milk?"

"I did not, but now they shall give no milk at all."

"Did you make our children disobedient and possessed?"

"I did not, but they shall be now."

The children in the court became hysterical.

"Have you consorted with and made a pact with the devil?"

"I did not, but I do now," she said, and stared at the judge, who turned into the devil.

"Did you swear allegiance on his book?"

"I have," she said, holding the Bible high above her head. Bats and dogs and cats flew about the room. The judge babbled ancient laws in ancient languages. All in attendance in the courtroom hallucinated, except the jury, who witnessed the power of evil. The witch stood like a natural disaster to be tried, judged, convicted, and punished.

"Ask me if I will destroy this miserable little town with all its miserable inhabitants," the witch in the dock laughed maniacally.

The jury screamed, "Innocent! This woman is innocent of being a witch, and we do declare that henceforth there will be no other trials, that there is no such person as a witch and no such thing as witchcraft."

"Then there is no need for me to continue being a witch,"

the accused said and repeated, "I am not a witch," three times. "Take warning, do not give anyone the right to kill for they shall surely kill you."

Two hundred people were released from prisons, and there was no more talk of witchcraft in Salem. In other parts of the world witch trials went on, but in Salem they stopped that day when they made a witch.

WITCH

The Professor found the monument to the Witch Trials. "Just another inane thing erected after every tragedy to assuage the conscience of officialdom. Three hundred years ago our legal system killed nineteen innocent people. This year the governor wants to reestablish capital punishment. He wants us to give his administration another chance to kill citizens again."

The Professor lectured us more about the great trading days of Salem. "Fortunes were made by many proud upstanding Yankees by privateering, rum, slaves, and perhaps a little drug traffic in the Orient. Not too respectable, but hell, you can always fund a church to regain respectability."

Returning to the boat we rowed away from Derby Wharf out into deeper water and anchored.

A little wine made palatable the indigestible aggregate the Pilot cooked. Each one found "his place," retired to it, and passed out, while our innards struggled to rid themselves of what we had ingested.

In the morning we said farewell to Salem and set sail for Cape Ann. We made our way out the narrow, shallow channel that finally caused the demise of Salem as a worldly commercial port. We sailed by Haste Shoal, Misery Shoal, between Beverly Farms and Great Misery Island into Manchester Bay, between House Island and Gales Point, inside of Kettle Island across Magnolia Harbor, Popplestone Ledge, and Norman's Woe into Gloucester Harbor, where we rounded Ten Pound Island and looked for a spot to anchor in the crowded harbor. We sailed up to the first mooring we saw, and the Waterman grabbed it.

"Decisions are easy when you don't care what you do," he said.

"Unless you meet the owner who doesn't care what he does in response," the Pilot warned.

The Professor began his historical dissertation by telling us that the little settlement of Gloucester had always been noted for fishing.

"And drinking," the Pilot added. "The more they fished the more they drank. The fish couldn't keep up and soon gave out. The fish houses became taverns." This revelation made the Assyrian and Waterman extremely happy.

We were given a lift into shore by a passing boat. A narrow street led us into the center of the prosperous little village of taverns. We separated, each to satisfy his needs. I purchased food at a local market, causing the merchant to stare in amazement at the quantity, not knowing what one man with five healthy spirits was capable of consuming.

It was apparent that the Pilot was correct about the town's renowned thirst. Almost every third shop was a tavern. In one of these establishments I met up with the Assyrian, Pilot, Waterman, Piscatologist, and Professor, observing the native custom of tippling.

When we returned to the shore we noticed another boat had rafted beside us. It proved to be a native of Nahant. Upon seeing us he came ashore in a small rubber raft and gave us a lift out to our boat. We discoursed convivially until dusk, in the course of which he explained that he was on his way back after having sailed to Rockport and thought he would loan us his raft since he had no further use for it. It was a welcome addition.

Next morning, shortly after his departure, we got underway. The Piscatologist threw over a dredge and hauled up an assortment of discardables. Not a living thing could be found. An indication of how efficient our technology has made us, and a good reason for the inhabitants of the defunct little village to drink.

We sailed by Ten Pound Island and cleared Gloucester Harbor by 8:00. As we made our way up the southeastern coast of Cape Ann,

TEN POUND

STRAIGHTSMOUTH

I wound the ten-dollar clock but, like myself, it refused to work. I shook it too vigorously. The hands fell off. I restored its appendages and put it gently aside to recuperate.

We passed close by Thacher's twin-towered lights, where insect-like fishing boats dotted the horizon. We sailed boldly through the narrow gut at Straightsmouth Island and into Sandy Bay. The clock started ticking again at Halibut Point.

TWIN LIGHTS

With the light southeasterly breeze we started at once for the Isles of Shoals, which lay nearly due north of us, about twenty miles away. The wind failed. Discouragingly, Cape Ann was still in sight astern of us at noon. We rowed until a whale surfaced nearby. "We didn't think anything was down there," the crew shouted, throwing their lines in the water.

"Pull those silly lines in, you damn fools. There isn't anything down here," the whale said. "I haven't eaten in weeks. You've depleted our food supply. You desperately try to reintroduce birds into this area, but how the hell do you think they can survive if there are no fish? You've had as much time to evolve as the rest of us and that's all you've managed to do is make yourself into a dismal failure," he continued. "You're really too stupid to do anything right, yet you still rationalize your existence with religion, politics, and science. You're not necessary. You're only necessary to yourself. Nothing else really needs you. In fact, everything on this planet could get along very well without you."

"I thought whales had better dispositions," the Professor told him.

"Anyone's disposition would deteriorate after witnessing what you donkeys are doing," the whale replied.

I felt a breeze. "You've brought the wind back," I shouted to the whale.

"You're hopeless," the whale said despairingly, and disappeared. The wind strengthened to a fine sailing breeze. Far off on the horizon, an immense ship appeared to be anchored in mid-ocean.

"That's the Isles of Shoals," the Pilot informed us. By midafternoon we sailed between Whiting Island Light and Star Island into hospitable Gosport Harbor. "The holding ground is bad and it is not advisable to anchor," the Pilot said.

WHITING ISL. LIGHT

So we secured the boat to one of the available moorings.

We cooked, ate, and inflated the raft. Paddling ashore the Pilot discovered that air was leaking out of the raft while the Waterman discovered that water was leaking in. At the dock a young man informed us that we were not allowed to land on the island after sunset. The sun had just set.

"Could we land to pump up our raft?" I asked.

"Can't permit it. Rules are made to be obeyed," the robot told us.

We quickly paddled back to the boat and climbed aboard, wet and angry. The Professor made hot chocolate and told us the strange history of the island's discovery. In the spring of 1614, while in the service of his king, John Smith made the first recorded visit to the island. Of course, Gosnold landed in 1602, Pring in 1603, Jones in 1604, Champlain in 1605, Black in 1607, Harrison in 1608, Smuttynose in 1609, Argal in 1610, Breakwind in 1611, Star in 1612, Appledore in 1613.

Still, Smith is credited with having discovered the islands in 1614, since he recorded them. The record, typically, disappeared. Immediately after the islands were discovered, an altercation ensued over naming them. Suggestions were asked for: Brown suggested, "Brown's Islands," Green suggested "Green's Islands," Cook suggested "Cook's Islands," Baker suggested "Baker's Islands," Carpenter suggested "Carpenter's Islands," Steward suggested "Steward's Islands." All six of the aforementioned men were flogged and put in chains until they agreed that Smith should name the islands after himself—as he did everything else they found.

Soon after Smith left, a castaway named Peter Shoal was washed ashore, reluctantly becoming the first permanent resident. He was heard only to refer to the islands as "my god-damn-pile-o-rocks." As a rhyme, it was generally thought to be inappropriate. In no time at all, a shore woman heard of his soulful solitude and sailed out with the intention of sharing his blissful solitude. She and he soon multiplied their solitude. And very soon you could not set foot on any of the islands without stumbling over a Shoaler. The islands were named after each of their adorable tribes, "Smuttynose Shoal," "Hog Shoal," "Shag Shoal," "Appledore Shoal," "Star Shoal," "Cedar Shoal," "White Shoal," "Lunging," "Malaga," "Duck," "Seavey," "Mingo," etc. Hence the "Isles of Shoals."

Next morning we paddled ashore again only to be told that we were now too early. "No one is permitted ashore until 10:00 A.M., and don't ask me to make an exception," we were told by another robotal Shoaler. We hastily paddled back to the boat.

The spirits dropped their linens over the side until 10:30, at which time we pumped up the raft again and paddled ashore. Not greeted by a Shoaler with rules this time, we wandered freely over the island. It was liber- ally adorned with grave- stones over Shoalers who obviously couldn't abide the rules.

A monument on the highest hill read, "Under this stone lies the remains of Reverend Tuck. Although a graduate of Harvard, he proved to be an affable man, polite in manner, amiable in disposition, of great piety, diligent and faithful." The Waterman rightfully wondered what his one great failing was that he had acquired at Harvard, for such a great mass of stones to be put on top of him.

Next morning the

Professor and I crossed over to Appledore to visit with ghostly Celia Thaxter in her famous parlor. She and her husband tended the lighthouse on Whiting Island for several years before retiring to Appledore to grow flowers and write poetry. We found no evidence of her island fairyland as she decribed it. The free pagan spirit had left with her demise. The wind and waves did not sing, but moaned; the sky did not smile down upon us, but frowned. The birds perched on rocks, sadly pensive. We sat about also waiting for some evidence of Celia's exultation. We found none and disappointedly paddled back to the boat.

We promptly set sail and quickly left that grim inhospitable collection of Peter Shoal's "god-damn-pile-o-rocks." The wind proved to be unsteady, demanding that we alternately row and sail. Stage Harbor was our destination, but the tide along the shore and the descending sun mocked our efforts as we reached the entrance to Cape Porpoise. Multitudinous lobster-buoys impeded the channel. But with the rudder attached to the full keel of our boat, we had no problem sailing over the impedimenta. We anchored on the outer line of boats.

A 12-foot gaff-rigged boat named *Ben Gunn* came alongside, luffing its loose-footed sail. The ragged, bearded occupant told us he lived on a derelict, washed up on Troff Island. He resided there contentedly with his wife and two children. We talked disparagingly of politics for a while. Before sailing away he invited us to visit his island when we found time.

BEN GUNN

We were awakened the next morning at 5:30 by lobster-boats hauling their traps around us. There was no wind. So we decided to stay another day and rest. The spirits went ashore to pig down fish, lobsters, and clams at the local Fang and Claw Eatery. They devoured whatever was put before them while talking of work, money, war, sex, old times, hard times, sickness, dying, and death. I dismissed myself by maintaining my sympathetic affinity with the sea and refusing to eat anything that came from it.

"But fish eat fish," the Piscatologist declared.

"That is their only source of food as you well know. It is not ours as you also well know. We are the only creatures that eat everything every other living thing eats."

"You live by too many rules," the Pilot said dismissing me.

I paddled out to Ben Gunn's Island. There was already a raft on the beach. Three men sat on the edge of the woods. I avoided them and walked along the shore after finding the undergrowth too dense to enter the woods. Circling the island I soon came across Ben Gunn's boat and camp. No one was about except for a deer, which stared at me for a minute then bolted into the brush toward the men. I waited for a gunshot. Nothing. So it was divinely decreed that the deer would not meet

DOE

a nut with a gun that day. I returned to the raft, picked up the crew in town, and paddled back to the boat. I poured a liberal ration of rum for all to lift their spirits. The Assyrian assiduously recorded it in the log.

The next day we sailed with a fair wind until mid-afternoon, when a fog rolled in from the sea. The Pilot asked where the radar reflector was.

"We have none," I told him.

"Then where is the fathometer?"

"We have none."

"Lead line? Horn? Bell?"

"None."

He found the binoculars; they had only one eye-piece. The Pilot expressed his regard for my seamanship with a stream of salty expletives. We continued as the wind held. Waves soon appeared off the bow, breaking on the rocky

FOG

shore of Richmond Island. Following the shore we heard the bell of the entrance buoy. Turning to port we found a beach and anchored. After sunset the fog lifted, whereupon we could see the safer anchorage behind Richmond Island. After sailing there we anchored snugly amid other boats. Although we sat beneath a clear, starry sky in a serene harbor, I did not sleep well that night, for I dreamt I was still working in that dismal Job I had resigned from, with all the desperate people trying to "hang in there." I awoke, grateful to be on my boat.

Next morning we found that a cold front had come through during the night, leaving strong winds to blow away the remnants of the morning fog. The Pilot, perched on the bow, had caught a fish and suggested we have it for breakfast. "Fish belong in the ocean. To be eaten by other fish. Throw it back." I demanded. "I do not want to appear unreasonable, but fish and meat shall not be eaten aboard this vessel."

The crew looked at each other, stunned, apparently by the clarity of my reasoning. "Fruits, vegetables, and grains shall be consumed on this vessel, not everything in creation."

The crew remained stunned. The Pilot and I plotted the

course to Jewell Island, while the crew plotted mutiny. It was ten miles and would take three or four hours at most.

We hoisted sails and got underway by 9:00, rounding close beneath the high cliffs of Cape Elizabeth. The breeze being fair and steady, we made a quick passage across Casco Bay, sailing into Jewell Island Harbor and anchoring before noon.

CAPE ELIZABETH

Admittedly it was still early, with an entire afternoon of good sailing ahead of us, but we could not decide where to go beyond where we were. So we decided to stay— which worked out badly. Leisure permitted mutinous irritability to fester. For days now the Assyrian's mouth had been continually chewing, making animal noises of appreciation. "Will you stop eating?" I finally demanded of him.

"Hungry," he mumbled through his chewing. "Haven't eaten in fifteen seconds."

The Pilot's pipe decided to abandon ship and went over the side. Perturbed, he paid out a steamy stream of profanity, ending with an oath to give up smoking forevermore. And forevermore subjecting us to the deterioration of his culinary skill, which we shortly sampled. The Waterman heaved the Piscatologist's specimens over the side, declaring, "They are crawling with vermin."

All this irritability, I suspected, resulted from our abbreviated day of sailing. I escaped by inflating the raft and paddling ashore with the Professor. We walked about the island while he named the plants and trees and birds and insects with such familiarity that I thought he expected them to acknowledge their names and strike up a conversation as with an old friend.

Being in a playfully thoughtful mood, I explained that "each object has individuality." I asked him, "How would you like to be referred to as just a member of a species?" And all he had named I rebaptized with deservedly dignified names: Wesley R. Weatherbee was a tree; Theresa Quimbly was a flower; Melvin J. Merryman was an insect; Desmond P. Romavonit was a seagull.

Needless to say, the Professor did not appreciate the spoof and returned to the boat much besmitten and much given to mutiny. Alone now, and not caring for my own company, I returned to the unhappy boat and found the sullen crew members avoiding each other. We ate silently, retired to our berths, slept soundly, and awoke the next day to raise the sails and hurriedly leave the ugly mood of that innocent little harbor. While sailing we discussed the previous day and concluded that we were all happiest when sailing and not tethered to the muddy bottom of a port where an uncheerful atmosphere could hang over us like a quarantine flag at the truck.

That day's sail proved to be well worth coming that far. The wind strengthened as we passed West Brown Cow and Webster Rock Light. "We should reef the main," the Pilot admonished.

"The weather changes rapidly during a day off the coast of Maine, and I anticipate the wind to fail soon, leaving us sitting idly on a glassy sea," I replied.

We raced along daringly under a full press of sail, the rigging complaining vociferously before we anchored in the lee of Seguin Bay at an hour after noon. "From where we're anchored the wind would blow us

SEGUIN

ashore in the raft, but we would never get back out to the boat, so there will be no going ashore," I explained to the crew.

"Then what's to eat?" the omnivorous Assyrian asked.

"Instant soup," the Pilot answered irascibly. "Green pea, chicken with rice, and broccoli with cheese. I've mixed them all together." I suggest the reader try this combination sometime for a really ugly experience. However, as a measure of the extent of our hunger, there were no complaints from the crew. They retired with this dunnage in their stomachs and slept with tranquil solemnity.

Next day, anticipating trouble, I brought the anchor back to the cockpit so I could heave it over from there. Then we sailed for Damariscove through thick fog and gusty winds. When we came to an island and tried to enter the harbor a lobsterman came out of the fog and asked what I thought I was doing.

"Entering Damariscove," I informed him.

"Damned if you will—there ain't no harbor there, and that ain't Damariscove. It's Outer Heron Island." He chuckled. "Damariscove is more easterly."

We sailed on and came to another island. Coasting along its shore we found an opening and sailed in to where we thought, again, the harbor should be. The fog lifted just as we dropped the anchor. Miraculously, we were in the inner harbor of Damariscove.

We rafted ashore and walked about the old abandoned fishing station. The wind blew unimpeded over the bleak and barren hills. It was truly beautiful to the eye like a desert or a mountain top but just as fearfully unlivable. The temperature dropped to 50 degrees that night, and the wind blew waves into the narrow harbor and bounced the boat and its weary occupants about all through the night.

Next day at sunrise, under a clear sky, we rowed out onto

a flat sea toward Monhegan. The Pilot worried about
our destination. "Will there be moorings at Monhegan?" the Pilot asked, "because I've been told that it
is not advisable to anchor."

"We'll find a mooring," I assured him
without knowing a thing about the island. The sea and sky were aflame with
the setting sun while Monhegan disap-

FLAT SEA —

peared and reappeared in the sea fog. We entered Monhegan
Harbor and tied up to one of three red guest moorings beneath
the great hotel.

We breakfasted the next morning, showered,
and washed clothes. Then we
hiked the trails through the
forest to the spectacular
eastern shore where high
rocky cliffs faced an unbro-
ken horizon.

When we returned, the
Artist insisted on taking us to
visit the resident painter. "We
were students together," he ex-

CLIFFS

plained. "We both were exceptional students in the school and
great things were expected of both of us. He went on with
single-mindedness to establish himself in the world of art while
I became lost in experimentation and indecisiveness," the artist
said apologetically. "Here I stand before you at the end of a
long and unproductive life."

The resident artist was overjoyed to see him. He offered us
food and drink and reminisced on old school memories. A long
discussion on art ensued. "Society will only tolerate what it
wants at the moment. All else is ignored," I heard them complain. "It worships dead cultures and does not provide fertile

ground for living inspiration to grow."

I left them struggling with the muse and visited the lighthouse museum where in my distrac-
tion I left my backpack. When I returned I found the bag outside the
door. Later I left the bag outside
a coffee shop and next morning found it again. The way-
ward bag played hide and
seek for the rest of our stay on

MUSEUM

the island. But since it was apparent that nothing moved on
the island, it was always found, much to its chagrin.

We paddled to Manana Island to see the runic writings,
vertical scratches on the face of a rock made by Vikings. The
locals say they are game scores.
Vikings 3–Indians 1.

RUNIC

"The weather was terrible before you came," we were told by
a local.

"We brought the good
weather, and we'll take the
good weather with us when
we leave," the Pilot told the local.

We sailed with the morning sunrise, making course
for Tenants Harbor. Wary of fog, the Pilot insisted on charting a course that took us
close to islands and markers along
the way. So we passed Allen
Island and Burnt Island, old
Culley Ledge, the Brothers
and Mosquito Island, then
between Southern and
Northern Islands to enter

BURNT ISLAND –

Tenants Harbor on a flooding tide. We regarded the boat as our home now and preferred staying aboard.

The next day, Sunday, we awoke to rain and strong wind; small craft warnings again. Not a boat had left the harbor. The Pilot advised us to stay also. We were confined to the boat most of the day until we got a ride to shore from a passing boat. We walked to the local quarry, which was the only attraction the town offered. There, the bones of Mother Earth were dug up to make our silly buildings and monuments. All the evidence of early explorers must have been quarried away. Inscriptions telling that Ships of Tarsus landed here. Carthaginians, Phoenicians, perhaps Egyptians, Saint Columbo, followed by Saint Brendan. All the inscriptions are gone, leaving a hole in the ground. Do we intentionally hide our past? It seems so, since we've destroyed every evidence of it.

QUARRY

Back on the boat we settled in for the night. I missed the classical music on the radio. It rained during the night providing a pleasant sound to sleep by. The rain had stopped by daylight, but the sky remained overcast. We were away at 9:00 to Rockland, thirteen miles away, with a tide favorably flooding eastward until 4:00. We were close hauled on a starboard tack for two miles, and then we sailed more freely to Whitehead Island Light. The strong tidal current earned us extra knots as we broad-reached Muscle Ridge Channel. Many large boats were

WHITE HEAD LIGHT

motoring in the opposite direction to us,
fighting both tide and wind. Poor devils.
We soon passed Otter Island and Owls
Head Light to anchor in Rockland
Harbor by the public ramp.
It rained again that night,
giving me less reason to
miss classical music.

MUSCLE RIDGE

In the morning the first thing we heard was a damn motor.
I hate motors. The crew hates motors. We hate the sound and
the stench of them. They go on brainlessly dominating our
lives. We are senseless victims of the
damn things. Cars, trucks,
buses, trains, planes—
I hate them all. "Why can't
an electric motor be developed with batteries as ballast?
No fumes, no noise. Charged by
solar, wind, magnet, water. And boats should be dry sailed with
no antifouling paint. Trailers or lifts in and out. They sit on
moorings day and night, not in use, fouling the water and in
danger all the time."

MORNING

"He's in a bad mood," the Artist warned the others. The
Professor turned the radio on to hear the election results.

"Elections are a fraud," I told him. "It's a shell game. We're
told that the solution to all social problems is under one of
the shells."

"But you have to make a choice," he
demanded.

"No, I don't, when I know the pea is
palmed," I said and went off to the library
to find out what day it was.

When I returned I wrote in the

LIBRARY

log, "The Captain brought rum aboard." To the delight of the Assyrian, we cheerfully imbibed from soup cans, for I had no cups.

I asked the harbormaster about the trawlers in the harbor. "Russians buying fish," he said. "We sell them only soft fish that's not used around here. It's good for them and good for us," he told me.

RUSSIAN FISH FACTORY SHIPS

"How is it good for us?" the Waterman asked.

"Is Maine for sale? If so, the Russians will buy it," the Pilot declared.

"A few Japanese ships will soon buy America, and the government will sell it to them," the Professor said.

We filled the glasses again and drank in silence pondering inevitables until the night closed over us.

The next morning the Assyrian wrote in the ship's log, "The Skipper drank copiously last night and drank again this morning." Which was true. The weather turned foul to match my mood. It began to clear by noon as we sailed out of the harbor on a light westerly wind. We rolled in the wake of boats leaving the harbor. There was a thick fog to the north as we passed Rockland Light. Off Isleboro the fog rolled over us and, not having taken an accurate compass course or seen a marker, I didn't know where the hell we were. We anchored near an island as the fog thickened.

"Where are we?" the Waterman asked.

"Frankly, I don't

ROCKLAND LIGHT

know," I replied confidently and broke out the rum and soup cans to stop the panic. In time, the fog lifted slightly, and we bumped along the islands into Dark Harbor, where we anchored and rafted into the Terratine Club.

"We have a strict policy," we were told.

"The cruising book says guests are welcome," I said.

"Guests of members," we were told.

"We came in because of the fog," I explained.

"Well, since no one is around to see if I enforce the rules, welcome."

"That's how Squanto greeted the Pilgrims," I told the crew.

There were fifty-five boats in the harbor, taking every mooring, and not one of them moved while we were there.

The night came on quickly with the fog, and we retired early. The next day we sailed out of Dark Harbor rounding Thrumbcap Island to starboard and headed northwest to the gap between Grindal Point and Warren Island. We could see the whitecaps caused by strong headwinds out into West Penobscot Bay. So we very sensibly came about and ran back down Gilkey Gullet, benefiting from the wind and tide. It was a wonderfully exciting sail through Job Island and Lime Island where the water shallowed to five feet into East Penobscot Bay toward Resolution Island.

RESOLUTION ISLAND

"This island," the Professor told us, "was fought over by the French, Spanish, Dutch, English, Indians, and Americans many times. They fought not to own it but to disown it. Whoever won the battle declared the island to be owned by the loser. Then the loser fought to disown it. As in all wars, the battles, ships and weapons, the admirals, generals, and politicians are written about in great detail, but history does not tell us the reason for fighting to disown the island. It remains one of the mysteries of the Maine coast."

The following wind and tide took us past Buck Harbor and Pumpkin Island Light. Twenty cruising boats with spinnakers flying accompanied us down Eggamoggin Reach. Another great sailing day. We passed a number of offshore islands where trees had been cut, burned, or sold, animals slaughtered, waters over-fished, stone quarried, soil eroded, leaving a dead island. It was then given to a conser-vation group to rejuvenate. How dead must an island be to be of no use?

We made our way to Western Cove on Stin-son Neck. We anchored,

DEAD ISLAND

paddled ashore, and hiked to the Haystack Art School. Built on the side of a cliff, the buildings were suspended above the ground by wooden pilings. The Artist became uncontrollable in that aerie, lecturing the teachers as well as the students. "You've learned to draw and paint reasonably well. Now what do you do with it? It is like learning to walk and talk. Where do you walk to? What do you talk about? Now that you can draw and paint, what do you draw and paint? Do you continue practicing just to show how well you can draw and paint, and walk and talk? Are you satisfied to walk better and talk better? What was the object of learning your craft? To merely do it, and try to do it better than everyone else? Think about it . . ."

A contest was ongoing with the motif of flags. The Artist was asked to submit something. He agreed and went into seclusion back aboard the boat. He brought his contribution ashore late that night in great secrecy. Next morning it could not be found, and he was asked where it was. "It is there," the artist explained.

"And when it is found it will show that Art is free, that it is not merchandise to be bought and sold, for it has no value. It is useful, to be used therefore and not to be preserved. It is commonplace and not to be stored in museums and private collections. And finally, it should be shocking, not appreciated and admired."

By day's end it was found, in the wash rooms. All the rolls of toilet paper had the flags of the world painted on them. The Artist was promptly asked to leave. His influence was too disruptive and anesthetic on the developing minds of the students. The Artist, of course, was baffled by the unappreciative reaction to his exhibit and had to be dragged back to the boat and held down.

A thick fog had settled over the harbor. The Pilot and I plotted a conservative course of short hops from buoy to buoy, the first being one-and-a-half miles to the edge of an island. We decided that we had better get out of that harbor, or we'd all be as crazy as the Artist. We raised the sails and pulled the raft aboard and raised the anchor. We then rowed out into the fog, making for the island. The fog never lifted. In time there was a slight breeze that had us dashing along finely through the fog. When the wind lightened we rowed, making slow progress, not wishing to come upon the land too quickly.

The boat never wanted to stay on course and continually wandered hither and thither as caprice impelled. During the entire voyage we could never get the boat to self-sail, even for a minute. Ten hours of sailing meant ten hours at the tiller. Later we discovered if we raked the mast aft slightly the boat gained a weather helm and proved more controllable. After sailing for an hour we came upon the expected island and sailed along its shore, rounded it, and found the first buoy. It had the wrong number on it, according to our twenty-year-old charts.

After a conference we decided the charts were wrong and the numbering of the buoy system had been reversed to intentionally confuse people using ancient charts. Confidently we

STONINGTON

changed course for the next buoy. The fog stayed with us. Boats motored past. Miraculously we found the next buoy and the next and the next until we approached the harbor of Stonington. The fog lifted slightly, enough to see boats at their moorings. We passed close by two moored schooners and anchored near the public landing, for no one wanted a long paddle ashore in a leaky raft. We ate something that was concocted by the irascible Pilot, tasteless and indescribable.

MOORED SCHOONER

CHOW

Looking across the thoroughfare we wondered why many larger boats were anchored on the other shore. We were soon to learn the reason. During the night the wind picked up—pitching and rocking the boat. The rigging began to scream. I lowered another anchor and noticed the rocks close astern.

"That's why the boats are anchored on the other side. They heard the weather and knew these winds were coming. We should have secured to a mooring farther out from these rocks," the Pilot said, always free with advice when it was too late.

"I hope the wind changes direction," I said with concern.

The wind didn't change direction, and the rocks were now four feet off the transom. The anchors dragged until the small anchor caught on a rock. The flooding tide saved us. We were now directly over the rocks that were exposed at low tide.

"If we put the mainsail up we will drag more," the Pilot said.

"I suggest we just raise the jib, pull the anchor, and hope the boat falls off to port, away from the rocks."

"If we fall off to starboard we'll be wrecked," the Waterman added.

The whole thing was not thought out too well, but if it had been we'd have been too scared to do anything. We did what we did, and the boat did the right thing.

"We're extremely lucky to have an intelligent boat," the Professor said.

We ran downwind to the dock, luffed the jib, and tied up. I heard a voice from out of the night say, "If you're from Nahant, you must know Tom."

"I'm Tom," I replied, exhausted.

"Then you'll have to visit us on our island. There's a mooring for the boat and a cabin for you to stay in."

"Where is the island?" I asked.

"Across the thoroughfare; Devil's Island it's called."

"I'm heading that way. If the weather doesn't improve, expect me."

"Good. See you there."

Our host boarded a Phil Bolger–designed boat, cast off from the dock, and sailed away like a duck in a breeze. Across the Deer Island Thorofare they disappeared between Green and Russ Islands.

Later that morning we hoisted sails, but in the thoroughfare the wind and waves were too strong to take on the beam so we turned and ran before it, rounding Russ, Camp, and Bold Islands, approaching Devil's Island from the east. We beat up the north side, logically thinking the moorings would be on the sheltered side of the island as the chart indicated. After twice striking rocks, the exasperated boat told us, "There's nothing up here, you damn fools!"

"Thank you," I acknowledged and came about. The Bolger boat came into view around the eastern shore, sailing pluckily toward us. The occupants told us where the mooring was. We found the float beneath the water and the pennant suspiciously short. We secured to it, and paddled ashore. Our host graciously provided us with food and drink while we celebrated a child's birthday party, after which we were shown a cabin to stay for the night.

We found it too spacious and stationary. We didn't sleep well. The spirits and I paced the floor. The Professor explained a bit of lore of the island's name. A small band of natives occupied one half of the island while the other half was settled by a small religious group. All went well until the minister tried to convert the natives. They had a confrontation.

"We do not worship a god," the natives said, "for he slaughters every living creature from the tiniest to the greatest with seeming indifference. He is the greatest mass murderer known to us. We are subjected to unnecessary suffering and pain as well as death. This is evil. And if he designed, created, and determined this, then he is evil. Evil can only be associated with the devil. We will not worship the devil obsequiously as you do."

The minister, in a fury, drove the natives from the island for, as he declared, "They were as beyond God's reach." The natives, henceforth, referred to the place as the island of the devil.

"Where do you get all this information?" the Waterman asked the Professor.

"I used to read a lot," the Professor answered. "Now I don't bother reading at all. I just make everything up."

Next morning we found the boat high up on the beach, leaning against a rock with the chain and mushroom beside it. Over a long period of time the chain had wrapped itself around the shaft of the mushroom, shortening itself. At high tide the boat pulled the mushroom off the bottom, and all floated ashore. Again the boat demonstrated its intelligence by picking a convenient rock and gently leaning against it. I rowed an anchor out into deeper water and waited for the tide to float us.

Our host, apologizing profusely, gave us a sumptuous breakfast and waved goodbye as we sailed swiftly away, waving back at that small angelic group on Devil's Island. We made our way eastward down the Deer Island Thorofare. We sailed through the sinuous York Narrows and Casco Passage across Blue Hill Bay to Bass Harbor head where a narrow inlet permitted us to round the southern headland of Mount Desert Island and make our way up the Western Way between Great Cranberry Island and Sutton Island, across Frenchman's Bay to Winter Harbor on the Schoodic Peninsula.

While anchored in Winter Harbor, we noticed a sign on shore. "Absolutely No Trespassing," it read, provoking a discussion on property. "Our laws have finally forbidden us to occupy the planet," the Professor explained. "Everything is owned by this vampirish system of banks and real estate agents."

"Until now, every dollar we make is paid out to a criminal system of loans," the Pilot said.

"All loans should be abolished, and everyone who occupies property should own it," the Artist protested.

"Unthinkable!" the Piscatologist exclaimed.

"It's been done in the past. We've been educated to accept this selfishly insane economic system of debts, loans, and serfdom. Originally the property was obtained by force of arms— which is theft. Tom Paine said, 'Authority and property which is obtained by force of arms is not legitimate and should be discontinued the moment force of arms cannot sustain it.'"

"Instead we pay homage to kings and governments and uphold the rights of property," the Professor said. Needless to say, we didn't go ashore, and long into the night declamatory shouting emanated from the boat.

From Winter Harbor the next day we beat past Mark Island at the harbor's entrance, rounded Turtle Island, and sailed out into the expanse of Frenchman Bay. A whale-watching boat headed for us, seemingly for lack of something to gawk at. Now we knew how whales felt being chased and stared at. We bobbed in the wake of the ship as it circled us and then sped away looking for something else to gawk at.

TURTLE ISL.

WHALE BOAT

Along the shore of Mount Desert, beneath Mount Champlain, we passed one of the ubiquitous Egg Rocks that lie along the coast of Maine. "The name told the shore people where to collect bird eggs," the Piscatologist told us.

EGG ROCK

We continued with a fine breeze outside of the Thrumbcap Island between the impressively high Ironbound and Porcupine Islands into Bar Harbor. We anchored near the club. Immediately the club launch came out to tell us we were too close to their committee boat. They wouldn't like us to be banging into it. They offered us a free mooring farther inside the harbor. The crew immediately complained of the long row to shore. I reminded them of the short row at Stonington where we almost lost the boat.

PORCUPINE ISL.

The Professor stayed aboard trying to listen to the ball game on the radio, but the boat, swinging at anchor, varied the reception so he would lose the sound at critical moments, leaving him cursing like a true sports fan. Why an educated man would listen to grown men playing children's games is beyond me.

Ashore, the Artist went to a public exhibition in the park, telling them no doubt they were doing everything wrong. **BALL GAME** The Professor found the library closed and complained that they were always closed whenever anyone wanted to use them.

I carried our dirty clothes in two sailbags to the laundromat. While they washed I rented a bicycle and rode over the island. I came back exhausted, grateful that the end of the trip

was downhill or I would never have made it back. The spirits asked why I was back so soon. "The bicycle got tired," I replied.

"We're running low on money again. How the hell do you make money?" I asked. "One month out and I spent two hundred dollars and haven't made a cent. We're left with not enough for a meal or a mooring. What should I do?"

"You'll have to sell the boat," the crew suggested. I went ashore and told other boaters my boat was for sale. When I came back aboard that night I found a note saying, "I am interested in buying your boat."

I met the buyer the next morning at a coffee shop. I told him the price was two thousand dollars or best offer. I started describing the boat. He said he had been aboard and examined it when he had left the note. He took out a notebook where he had listed everything that was wrong with the boat. He then complained about all the work he would have to do.

"Working on a boat is fun." I told him. "I should charge you for all the fun you'll have fixing it up."

"I don't fix up boats."

"Then every true boater has friends who'll do the work for the sheer joy of it."

"How's the motor?" he asked.

"What motor? It's a sailboat. Doesn't need a motor."

"It should have a motor."

"If you want to motor around, buy a car. We've been sitting here talking for an hour, and you've never said what you're willing to pay for the boat."

"Well, I know a fellow who bought a boat like yours for $1,200 with a motor, loran, depth find . . ."

"Cut out the bullshit and make an offer."

"Now, don't get mad when I do."

"I'm mad already."

"I couldn't possibly offer any more than seven hundred dollars."

"Bullshit!"

"Don't get mad," he said.

"Why shouldn't I get mad?"

"Well, why don't we talk about sailing?"

"I'm through talking."

Later that night we cast off the mooring and rowed to another spot in the harbor. A pram came out of the dark and someone said, "Hello, Tom."

Still irritated and with a slight suspicion who it was, I said, "Who the hell are you?"

"I'm the fellow who offered to buy your boat. Why don't you come aboard my boat for a drink?"

I didn't like him, but I was curious to see his boat and maybe drink his booze. When I finished anchoring I climbed aboard his pram, and we rowed over to a 30+ Lugens. Once aboard he talked about his trip down the inland waterway to Florida.

"Why the hell did you want to buy my boat when you have this thing?" I asked.

"Well, a group of Typhoon owners are getting together to form a racing club, and I thought I'd join them."

Even with this plausible explanation I still regarded him as a used car dealer. Buy cheap and sell dear.

"That's how you make money," the spirit crew told me later.

"Money is not related to anything; work, thought, productivity, creativeness. It is acquired now by some mysterious paper-pushing process," the Professor said. "The people here have already made their money. This is the new breed."

I brought out the rum for the last time, which the Assyrian reported immediately in the log for the last time. We toasted the end of the cruise. Each crew member in turn told me what they thought of me—all being in agreement that I was the biggest pain in the ass they ever had the misfortune to sail with. I laughed idiotically as the descriptions got worse. They eventually gave up, realizing that no one could penetrate the shell of stupidity that encased me. We sat in silence and drank.

I related the story of the Caliph of Abdalrahman, the Mightiest Moorish Monarch of Spain. "He declared at the close of his life that he hadn't enjoyed one damn moment of it." As for my part, being not quite that hard to please, I admitted enjoying some moments of the cruise despite the problems and disappointments and constant bitching. The Professor, Pilot, Piscatologist, Waterman, and Artist grudgingly agreed that many happy days befell our lot; but, as with the poor people of Spain under the domination of the Caliph, the happiest was this day when they would leave the vessel and forever rid themselves of my insufferable presence. Whereupon the spirit crew left, leaving me alone with my insufferable self.

Fishtale

The old man sat in an ancient chair surrounded by discarded fishing gear. A young man stood by a small woodstove that took the chill out of the room. "So you want a story about the storm, young feller?" said the ancient man-chair.

"That's right," the young man replied. "A human interest story with the storm as a background."

"Tell you what, why don't you pour yourself a cup of coffee over there and let me think a bit."

"Fine; when you're ready I'll turn on this recorder."

ANCIENT
CHAIR-MAN

The old man-chair puffed on his pipe and stared into the distance. Finally he asked, "Do you know much about sailing, young man?"

"No, not much."

The old man chuckled behind his pipe and went back into deep thought. After a while his thoughts came back into the room. "Well, there's a story that happened

DEEP THOUGHT

166

during the storm. You can take it for what it's worth."

"Just a minute." The reporter snapped on his recorder and spoke into it. "This story is told to me by a native Nahanter as truthfully as he can recall."

HARBOR

The old man began. "This little harbor was crowded with boats. Lobster trawlers, longlining draggers, seineing scallopers, pleasure boats; dromons and carracks, hoogars and botters, hookers and hogboats, koleks, ulaks, and umiaks; mulettas, brawleys, scaffies, gyassas, gozoes, and xebecs; williwas and dollops. All firmly secured with extra brummel hooks and sea anchors, and flying yellow storm burgees. Everybody was waiting for the big storm headed this way. This harbor is open to the southern quadrant and is reasonably safe, but it was always best to worry

BLACK NUN

a bit. All the fishermen were right here in this room having a meeting.

"At the same time, a small sailing dory passed the black belled nun at Joe's Beach. It beat wing on wing among the boats until the sailor leisurely picked up the rhumbline from his mooring and spliced it to the Charlie Noble, then shipped the rudder and lowered the leeboard. Put the sails full and by. Intied the lubber line to his scow and piped himself aboard and skegged over to another dory that was sunk to the trunnels. The sailor lit his hawsepipe while examining this boat. Taking up a drogue, he bailed until the boat was dry, then looked for a limberhole or a lubberhole. Finding none, he secured the cockcombing futtock and swagged the scow for the dock. Leaving it adrift, he walked angrily into this room. The meeting had just ended. The fish-buyer was just saying, 'Is there anything else to be said?'

SWAGGING

THE ROOM

"'I have something to say,' the sailor said with hard tack.

"'Then go right ahead and say what's on your mind, young man.'

"'I have two sailing dories in the harbor. I've had them here for several seasons. This season they've been swamped, rammed, and vandalized. They're well out of the commercial traffic, so it makes me believe it's not accidental. I want to know who's doing it.'

TWO DORIES

"'We talk fish business here. Go to the harbormaster with your complaint,' a fisherman said.

"'I think some of you know who's doing this,' the sailor said.

"'We all know one another and we help each other. We do not help you,' the fisherman said.

"'This is a criminal act. What makes any of your boats safe?'

FIGHT

"'You do not belong on the sea. The sea is a livelihood, not a playpen for a baby. Boats are sailed to catch fish, not to play games with. Get out or I will fight you.' The fisherman moved at him threateningly.

"'Fighting settles nothing. But since no one wants to clear this up, we can settle it with the toy boats. You're all hiding your motorized monsters from the weather that's coming. My toy boats have been known to stand up to it. I'll challenge any one of you great fishermen to sail out around Shag's Light and back using my toy boats. It'll prove their sea-worthiness and your courage, rather than fighting,' the sailor said, staring truculently at the fisherman.

"'I will sail your toy. I will beat you in this weather. I will beat you twice. After the race I will beat you with my fists,' said the fisherman.

"'We'll see. The boats will be at the landing in the morning at 0700, regardless of the weather. And I'll put up two hundred dollars to tempt your greed if your courage fails.' The sailor left the room.

"The fishbuyer finally spoke. 'Well, we've heard him, and we all know who's been damaging his boats. I don't know why you've been doing it, but it's up to you to settle it.'

"'I will. You'll see. I'll beat him good.'

"'If you don't want to sail, we can get somebody else.'

"'Who? Who can sail like I can? I sailed these toys as a child. I'll show him what sailing is. No one else. I will go.'

"'Then that settles it. You'll meet him at the dock in the morning, and we'll take up a collection to match his two hundred dollars.'

"'Hah, for four hundred dollars I will race him to hell!'

I WILL RACE TO HELL

"'With this weather making up the way it is, you may very well have to.'

"The next morning when the two men met on the dock, there was no sun, and great seas broke at the harbor entrance. The wind rose in pitch and strength. A small group of men examined the boats and discussed the race.

"The fishbuyer spoke. 'As I understand it, you both start at the dock when I say, sail out around Shag's Light, be seen by the keeper, and return to the dock. The first one back wins. If either one of you doesn't want to race, now's the time to speak up. The weather's bad and it's going to get worse.'

"There was no response from the sailor or the fisherman.

"'Very well, the race officially starts now,' the fishbuyer declared, checking his dogwatch. The two men climbed into their boats."

CLEAR SO FAR?

The old man paused in his story and puffed on his pipe. "Have any trouble with the story so far, young man? Anything you want explained?"

"No, the story's great," the reporter replied.

"Well, let me tell you something about the Nahant Dory. It's usually

SPIT

16 FEET

16 feet long from stem to bow, but never truly; measurements were rarely used.

The length of each boat was as far as they could spit that day. They were built by the three Dory brothers, named Pitch, Roll, and Yaw, French-Canadians who settled in Nahant in the 1800s. When they began fishing in the spring, the story goes, they tore their houses apart and made boats. In the fall, they broke the boats up and repaired their houses for the winter.

Roll - PITCH & YAW

SPRING

FALL

"Made to be loaded with fish, each boat needed eight hundred pounds of cobblestones, called prayer books, for ballast to stay upright. As the fish were caught, the stones were thrown overboard. One fish, one stone . . . They had to be quarried and shaped. There was a strange connection between the stones and the fish. If the stone wasn't weighted and shaped right, the fish wouldn't bite. Many a ship came home still filled with prayer books of the wrong shape and weight. Boston's streets were paved with those bad stones, while the good ones paved the fishing banks.

"The transom of the boat was shaped like a tombstone. The

ONE FISH - ONE STONE

dorymen's names were carved into the transoms. When the men were lost, the boats were almost always found. When the boats were dismantled for the homeward voyage, the transoms were stuck into the ground at any convenient landing. Each ship

carried a goodly supply of transoms in the galley, and you'd often catch yourself staring at your own name as you ate, reminding you how close you were to the everlasting.

TRANSOM

THE EVERLASTING

"The sail in the dory had so many reef points it could be brought down to the size of a man's shirt. Beyond that,

you had two pair of hackmatack oars that were balanced like throwing knives . . . to beat the fish off when the boats were loaded and you had to haul in the lines.

"That's enough details about the boat; let's get back to the story," the reporter interrupted.

BEATING OFF THE FISH

"Details are important, young man. You should pay attention to details," the old man chided. "But I'll get back to the story."

"The sailor and the fisherman lost no time brailing their jibs and clewing their gollywobblers. Lubberlines were cast off. Both boats goosewing jibed and headed for the entrance of the harbor. The fisherman frapped his kite and kedged his scantlings while the sailor tommed up and furled by, disappearing into fiddlersgreen beyond the harbor. The fisherman scandalized his

boat. Waited and watched. Then pitch-poled the
boat about and tumblehomed
back to the dock.

GOOSEWING THEIR
GOLLYWOBBLES

"'Why did you come
back?' the fishbuyer asked.

"'I saw that nothing
could survive out there,'
the fisherman explained.

"'I did not think that you intended to go.'

"'I did not think that he would go until I realized he was mad.'

"'Why did you lead the man on?'

MADMAN

"'To get rid of him and his
damn boats. Good riddance. It
was his choice. He said he knew
the sea. The sea is cruel. I will
not fish ever again if he re-
turns, but I think that is the
end of that madman.'

"'I wonder. Madmen do strange things.'

"For the remainder of the day the wind was furious and
the sea became wilder. Trees were uprooted. The church steeple
toppled. Boats broke loose, smashed against one another, and
broke up on the rocks. The eye of the storm passed directly
overhead. The wind shifted 365 degrees. It was the worst storm
any living Nahanter had ever experienced.

THE EYE

"Next morning a small sail appeared in the entrance of the harbor. The townspeople stopped cleaning up their wreckage and stared in disbelief. They watched the boat approach the dock. It was in shambles. The hounds were athwartship. The partners were moonsheered. The whipstaff was snaffled. Even the pintles were gudgeoned. When he came alongside, he stepped ashore and frapped the rhumbline to a convenient baggywrinkle. No one made a move to assist him. He paid them no mind, walking up the ramp and into this room. The fishbuyer was there.

SMALL SAIL

"'That was quite a feat, young man,' he admitted.

"'It's better than brawling, and it shows that my boats are as good as any in the harbor,' the sailor replied.

"'Well, we've talked about that while you were gone and agreed anyone found damaging boats will be caught and held accountable.'

"'That's all that I ask.'"

"And, that's the end of the story," the old man concluded.

"Did he ever explain how he did it?"

"Nope, but the keeper at Shag's Light reported that a small sailing craft had laid in the lee of the lighthouse during the storm."

"And the fisherman?"

"Those are his slickers

LEE OF THE LIGHT

HISTORY?

hanging on that hook. Don't expect they'll be used again."

The reporter snapped the recorder off. "Thanks, old man. We just wrote a bit of history."

The old man sat alone afterwards and mumbled to himself, "Is that the way history is written?"

Whale Watching

in a Small Boat

The old man appears again as I'm loading the boat at the Dory Club Dock. "Going on another trip?" he asks.

"Yes." Then something makes me add, "I'd like to see the whales." Why did I say that? I only intend to sail out to the islands in Boston Harbor, not go chasing whales.

"When are you coming back?" the old man asks.

"I don't know." I reply. What am I saying? I do know. I'm just sail-

THE OLD MAN

ing for the day. The old man smiles and casts off my bow line. "Good luck."

ARROGANT BOAT

It is 9:00 in the morning. Too late to go on a long sail. Besides, I don't have enough food and supplies—although I did bring a sleeping bag; I don't know why. The sky is clear and the wind strong from the southwest. A perfect wind for Gloucester. There is no struggle of minds or conflict of intentions

outside the harbor. The boat arrogantly turns its transom on the islands of Boston Harbor and runs before the rising wind. I am Gloucester bound, like it or not. Shanghaied by the boat again!

I am told to turn on the radio, so as not to dwell on my captivity too much. I find it and turn to an FM station—a symphony by Haydn at full volume as twenty boats with spinnakers set race out of Marblehead and chase me off their course. By 2:00 P.M. I am at Gloucester. I sail into the harbor as far as I can and discover the Sevens Club, tie up among the big boats, and then can't find anybody. I can't even get off the dock because everything is locked up. I return to the boat and begin rowing away. When I look back, someone comes out the door of the club, so I turn and row back. When I find him, he is standing on the biggest boat I have ever seen. It would take at least ten strong people to handle it. He tells me that this is a private club and that there is a fish pier

PRIVATE

down the way a bit that would probably let
me tie up. I row away, chagrined, and then
raise the sails and beat to the end of a small
bay where the fishing boats are. I ask if it
will be all right if I leave my boat there for
a few hours. "Sure, nobody touch it; nobody use that space."

NOBODY TOUCH BOAT

I find a pay phone and call home.

"I'm in Gloucester."

"Good," the phone replies.

"But I'm coming home."

"Why are you coming home?" the phone asks.

"I left my little green pills there, and I don't have half the
gear I should have. And besides, the car is parked over at the
Dory Club, and it can't be left there overnight. I'll catch the
train here, and someone can pick me up at the station and drive
me to the club for the car."

"All right. Phone when you get to the station."

"Right."

I leave the pay phone and walk in every direction and ask
every person that happens along, "Where is the train station?"
Finally, I ask a gas station attendant who tells me, "The shortest
way is to run down those tracks and you'll meet the train." So, I run
down those tracks and come to a small group of people waiting.

"What time does the train come?"

"It doesn't come. The tracks are being repaired. You catch the bus here."

"What time does the bus come." FOUR

"I don't know. It's never on time." HEADED

"How much does it cost?" HYDRA

"Nothing."

Four men stagger out of a bar, talking about
fishing and looking like a four-headed Hydra.

178

"I should have had a camera," one man keeps repeating.

The bus arrives forty-five minutes late as I'm debating whether I should go back at all. Just before the bus arrives (I don't know if it's the late early bus or an early late bus) I find on the ground a leaflet about whale watching.

The bus door opens and I pile in with the drunken Hydra. "Is anyone getting off at Beverly Farms? Manchester? Danvers—?" the driver barks.

"No!" the drunks yell in unison.

"I don't want to hear nos; I want to hear yeses," the driver says truculently.

"Anyone have a yeah?" asks one of the heads. "Nobody has a yeah, driver." "What's that noise?" the driver asks, then declares, "If that ain't a flat, I'll eat my hat!"

WHAT'S THAT NOISE?

Another delay, I think to myself as the bus stops at a train station in Salem. "Does this bus go to Lynn?" I ask.

"This is as far as this bus goes, mister," is the reply.

"There isn't a bus to Lynn? I see buses in Lynn that come here. Don't they have to go to Lynn to come back here?"

"All I know is that there ain't no bus to Lynn."

"Is there a train to Lynn?"

"No."

"Then how do I get to Lynn?"

"That's your problem, buddy."

I get off the bus and hear someone ask, "Where does this train go?"

"I don't know," several people tell him.

NOTHING GOES TO LYNN!

"Get your tickets in the office before you board the train!" the conductor yells. As I'm making a phone call, the train pulls out with people running after it angrily screaming at it to stop.

"Hello," the phone says.

"I can't get a ride," I tell it. "Can our daughter pick me up in Salem?"

"No. She hasn't come home from work yet."

"Well, I'll start walking to Peabody and phone later." I hang up and start running and walking, alternately. In Peabody I phone again.

"She's not home yet," the phone tells me.

"When she comes in, tell her I'll meet her halfway."

"Don't go beyond the gelatine factory or she'll never find you."

I start walking again. At the gelatine factory, there's no daughter, so I continue on until I can phone again. "She just left to pick you up," I'm told. I'm past the gelatine factory now and hope that she doesn't pass me by. I start walking in the street so she'll see me and am almost home when she picks me up. From there, she drives me to Nahant to pick up the car.

"I thought you were sailing in Boston Harbor!" I hear.

"I was, but the wind was blowing just right for Gloucester, and the boat just . . ."

"I don't believe that."

"I do!" my son says, "That's Dad . . . any way the wind blows, the boat goes!"

"Will you drive me back to Gloucester?" I get an angry look and the great big "Damn!"

"Then I'll take the bus. I

FOUND

180

know they go there. They don't come here, but they go there."

"No, I'll drive you back," she says resignedly.

I gather up food, charts, binoculars, tent, and pillow and add an apple as an afterthought. On the way, I stop at a store for more food. When I come out of the store the wife is talking with a friend. "Now you can wait for me," she says.

"Fine. Does she want to come with us?" I suggest. The friend is agreeable, and we pile into the 1962 Dodge Lancer. I drive, and all the way they talk about psychic predictions, astrology, and the future.

RETURNING

I stop at the Whale Watch Restaurant in Gloucester and ask where the boats go to see the whales, Jeffrey's Ledge or Stellwagen Bank? I'm given a blank stare—no one knows a thing. "This is just a restaurant. We have nothing to do with the whale watches—that's just our name." I leave the restaurant and drive around the area where I thought I left the boat. I can't find it. Perhaps it's been moved or stolen. Now I don't even recognize the area where I thought I left the boat. I stop the car in disgust. I don't know where to go. I've lost the boat. I stare ahead despairingly, and the top of the mast appears above a wall. "Hey! That's it!" The boat has found me (Somebody has moved it. There is a fishing boat where I left it.)

IT FOUND ME!

I jubilantly climb down the slippery ladder and row the boat to the pier, throw in my gear, say good-bye, and row out into the darkness to find a moor-ing while the wife and her friend TO FIND A MOORING talk of psychic phenomena and drive away.

Someone yells, "Hey, mister, put some running lights on." I tie a flashlight to the mast just as I run over something in the dark. The boat stops. I feel the object with an oar. It has a ring in it. It must be a mooring. I tie up, pitch the tent, roll out the sleeping bag, and sleep soundly till sunrise.

After the usual preparation, I raise the sail and start out of the harbor. The wind is blowing like hell, so I pull into a small cove, tie up to a dock, and put a double reef in the mainsail. Reluctantly, I cast off on a strong southwest wind that whips up whitecaps. In time the wind eases off, and I begin to think of food. I'm getting sick of water, granola, and peanuts. I search for the apple and can't find it.

LOOKING FOR THE APPLE

I go through every bag over and over again. It isn't there. I remember distinctly putting this apple in one of the bags. I give up and begin to bail, sponge out the remaining water, and look for the leak. No luck. Will this boat ever stop leaking? "Perhaps if you were the equivalent age, you'd be leaking, too," the boat seems to answer. "Besides, it gives you something to do."

By 1:00 P.M. I am searching for whales in earnest. A whale watch boat passes, crowded with people, and everyone in it waves.

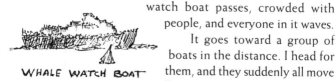

WHALE WATCH BOAT

It goes toward a group of boats in the distance. I head for them, and they suddenly all move off. "Forget it," I say to myself. "I've got to get back." I see the boats group up again. "Something must be there," the boat says. "We've come too far not to see a whale." The boats move off again. We pursue with determination and catch them just as bagpipe music starts playing on the radio. I turn the volume up and sail in among the whale watchers. "That's right!" the boat says, "Make a spectacle of us. It must be a 'bonnie' sight to see a single person in a small plaid boat sailing fifteen to twenty miles from land with bagpipes playing!"

WHALES

Three whales surface beside us, expelling air, then sound. I become more concerned about the whale watch ship that bears down on me, trying to get closer. I move off. The whales surface near me again. Boy, are they big . . . and impressive. The whales move slowly through the water as though they are so powerful that they can slow time down. I move farther away, and the whales don't reappear. It was a quick sighting and, you'd think, hardly worth it. But it was. There's something unexplainably strange about whales. The boat is silent. I turn away, leaving ten boats searching for the elusive whales.

I have no idea of my position. I take no dead reckoning. There is nothing here to take bearings from. "Well, what do we do now?" I ask the boat. "We find something," it replies. "It'll be interesting to see where we come out."

I look for the leak and then for the apple, and don't find either. It's great sailing but getting dark, with nothing in sight. I'm beating west by northwest, rolling in the swells with Chopin on the radio. It's overcast, and when it gets dark it will be "completely" dark. I search for the apple again. Can't find it. A two-masted schooner overtakes us, waves, and sails on. It's as dark now as I imagine it can get with a half-moon occasionally coming out from behind the clouds. The wind lightens. Then a strong gust hits the sail from another direction. I panic and drop the main. The wind lightens again, and I cautiously

raise a double-reefed mainsail. A faint
white flashing light appears ahead.

It must be Thatcher's Lighthouse.
A fishing trawler soon appears and
makes for the flashing light. It must be the
harbor. But where is Thatcher's? On the
chart it reads a red flashing light.
Off to starboard is a barely visible
red flashing light. Other boats

FLASHING LIGHT

follow the trawler in. I'm beating against the wind and can't follow directly. An outgoing tide is knocking me back. It takes a
long time to reach the light. Meanwhile, I tie a flashlight to
the tiller facing aft for a stern light. I hold the red and green
running lights in my free hand because every time I secure
them to something they go out. I have to shake them until they
go on again. I round the light and break-
water and search for a mooring, sailing
in among the boats and hoping
no one will notice us.
I eventually find the only
one available, but it doesn't
have a mooring pennant.
Not even a ring. I pull the line

ROUND THE LIGHT

up beneath the float and tie to it. Perhaps it's not good seamanship, but I'm too tired to play around. I retire at midnight,
sleep soundly, and awake at 8:30 to search desperately for the apple, only to have granola
again for breakfast. The wind is blowing
pretty hard now from the northeast, so I decide to reef the main but keep it lowered
and just run with the jib. I cast off.
The boat spins in place, then runs
madly out of the harbor.

CAST OFF

FETCH

The farther I get from land the longer the fetch and the bigger the waves. I try to stay close to the shore, then vaguely remember seeing rocks on the chart in this area. I check. Sure enough, there they are on the chart. This should be a red nun coming up. It isn't—it's a black can, Number 5. I'm in front of the Inner Breakers. I can't turn the boat. The waves will turn me over. I've

THE BLACK CAN

AMONG THE INNER BREAKERS

got to go through. There's a group of three rocks to the right, two rocks to the left. One rock ahead. Let's go straight ahead and try to miss the single rock. Better odds. All the rocks are under water, and the waves are breaking all around us from the wind. They have high crests and deep troughs. The center-board is up. I take a range on Halfway Rock and the black can I just passed. The line goes directly over the single rock. "We have to stay to one side to miss it," I tell myself. Soon I take another range on the smoke stacks of Salem and Halfway Rock and discover that I have passed the rocks. I've got to run out of luck soon, and then I won't be safe from disaster in a monastery. The wind is up to 30 knots.

The waves are getting bigger and cresting. Past Satan's

Rock, eighteen sailboats come out of
Marblehead, chasing after me.
I can't turn. I'm out of
control if I do. This
boat isn't supposed to
plane, but it sure is planing now. Sometimes the bow

SATAN'S ROCK

wave is directly under me. There is a lifting
sensation and a long hissing sound. The
boat is having a hell of a time. I am, too,
but am more wild-eyed and scared. We
round Eastern Point at Nahant and
eventually get safely in the
lee of the land. Should I
raise the main just for show
before we come in view of the
club? No, I'm too grateful to be alive

PLANING

to pretend, so we sail into the harbor and up to the dock con-
servatively under jib. And who is the first one to greet us? The
spectre.

YOU MADE
IT BACK

"You made it back, I see."

"Just about," I reply.

It is 1:00 P.M. We've sailed twenty
miles in four-and-a-half hours. Pretty
good for a small boat. As I unload the
supplies from the boat, the apple rolls
out and sits triumphantly on the dock.

THE APPLE